Retirement is For Younger People
Life is too short to retire

By Raymond Monbiot

Published in 2012 by

Raymond Monbiot, Eastgate House,
Burnham Market, Norfolk PE31 8HH

© Raymond Monbiot

ISBN 0-9542567-3-5

ISBN 978-0-9542567-3-9

Typesetting:
Raymond Monbiot

Printed by:
Barnwell Print Ltd
Dunkirk
Aylsham
Norfolk NR11 6SU
Tel. 01623 732767

CONTENTS

Introduction

The title of this book was inspired by Dr Kevin Brown, for twenty years a general practitioner and then medical adviser in the asbestos industry. He was expert in the relative dangers to health of different sorts of asbestos and the author of best- selling medical books dealing with the doctor/patient relationship. On 'retirement' he became one of the foremost growers of and authorities on heritage apples and pears about which I interviewed him for a local magazine when he was ninety years of age. He was as active and motivated as ever, having rediscovered and regenerated a heritage apple called 'Apple Dumpling'. With its thin skin it was ideal, wrapped in pastry, for agricultural workers to eat in the fields for a midday meal. He had recently accepted that he could no longer climb the highest ladders to prune his trees but when I asked him if he planned to retire he replied that he had come to the conclusion that 'retirement is a job for younger people'.

His great enthusiasm and sense of mission for his apple project were bringing him joy and satisfaction and keeping him active and engaged. Saving a variety thought to be lost and the continued quest for others were exciting and motivational.

Thinking about this I realised that some of the most valued members of the community are well into their seventies and eighties and continue to share their energy and talent with others of all ages. Some use their expertise from their days of employment. Others do something quite different. Had they done so during their employment years it would have been described as a career change. After 'retirement age' it might be described as 'active retirement', but why use the concept of retirement at all?

Continuing with one's career is of course not an option for professionals who are obliged by law to give up at a specified age - solicitors, doctors, High Court judges, for example. However, there is nothing to prevent them picking up another activity and enabling a less obvious talent to blossom. Most people have an unused skill, however unexpected. The paediatrician who gave up his career to enter TV's *Master Chef* has developed a business making high- quality cakes. The splendid Roger Bannister, now eighty- three and the first man to run a four 4 minute mile, became one of the world's leading neurologists and has seen at first hand what can be achieved in later life. He observes:

"I know several doctors who after their retirement have plunged into dangerous areas of the world and given their expertise, teaching, research and care. I admire their altruism wholeheartedly and pay tribute to *The Times/Sternberg Active Life Award honours.**"

He highlights Colin Murray Parkes, Britain's leading expert on bereavement. He had a distinguished career as a psychiatrist and worked closely with Dame Cicely Saunders to set up the hospice-based bereavement service. After being 'forced to retire' from clinical practice at the age of sixty-five, Colin Murray Parkes embarked on a second career exploring the links between grief, terrorism, violence and reconciliation and urged those in his position to resist 'the lure of the golf course' and make use of their retirement. 'Life is too short for retirement. I can understand people whose work is not particularly rewarding wanting to stop, but I think you use it or lose it,' he says.

Some of the most knowledgeable members of the community who are willing to share their expertise well into their eighties have escaped the popular perception that active life ends at retirement. But these really interesting people are prepared to share what they have learned and keep others active and motivated. They have left behind the younger people who have retired to their armchairs, bored, counting their ailments and waiting to die, and who often, sadly, have a preoccupation with the main regrets most common in old age. These regrets have been studied by numerous experts and observers and tend to fall into five categories.

- *(See website inspirationandchai.com/regrets-of-the-dying. html)*

1.   I wish I'd had the courage to live a life true to myself, not the life others expected of me.

2.   I wish I hadn't worked so hard.

3.   I wish I'd had the courage to express my feelings.

4.   I wish I had stayed in touch with my friends.

5.   I wish I'd let myself be happier.

Many did not realise that happiness is a choice but fear of change had them pretending they were happy. With retirement, if one wishes, the brakes come off, the hangups can fall away. Lost dreams can be rediscovered – at least some of them. It's not too late and it is surely better than sitting brooding over what might have been.

*Acknowledgement to The Times/Sternberg Active Life Awards.

1.
Tim Ambler

Tim Ambler is, or rather was, one of the giants of marketing. Never afraid to challenge established thought he achieved a highly respected reputation. He has that capacity to think and express what many believe are unreasonable thoughts but it is unreasonable people who change the world. His humour has done much to win over less iconoclastic colleagues.

Fearless determination served him well in national service. The authorities gave him the choice of Salisbury Plain or Cyprus but he argued successfully that he would be more useful in Singapore which he had known from childhood. The War Office, as the Ministry of Defence was then, was not known for its flexibility so it was to everyone's surprise that he was posted as requested and found himself, at nineteen years old, managing transport, butchers, bakeries and fuel supplies about which he knew little or nothing. 'I was in frequent trouble for minor infringements of regulations.' Useful experience of what was to come!

After national service he went up to St John's College, Oxford, in 1957 and graduated in mathematics three years later. The next stage was articles with Peat, Marwick, Mitchell, slightly delayed by being part of a quartet who drove a busload of undergraduates to Turkey and back. The insurance company took some persuading that driving an armoured car qualified one to drive a bus. After qualifying as a chartered accountant in 1963, he joined International Distillers and Vintners (IDV) as an accountant in the fine wines division and subsequently rose to General Manager of the division's supply operations. National service did have advantages.

"In 1968 the government generously funded my master's degree, the equivalent of an MBA at Massachusetts Institute of Technology. I was sacked by IDV in the course of negotiating my unpaid leave of absence, not very diplomatically it would seem. They relented to the extent that if I could complete the two- year course in half the time, I would be re-employed."

One thing Ambler learned at MIT was the blindingly obvious point (to marketers at least) that spending the money was a lot more fun than counting it. He left IDV as an accountant and returned, according to him, as a marketer. The company took the risk and appointed him Marketing Director of the main UK company.

"They say that marketing is the most fun one can have in business with one's clothes on. My main responsibility was to revitalise Smirnoff vodka which had been stuck on 300,000 cases a year through the sixties. After a few false starts, Young and Rubicam, the ad agency, struck gold with 'The effect is shattering' campaign. Older readers may recall 'I was an accountant until I discovered Smirnoff...The effect is shattering.' It did have its troubles. The IDV board wanted the campaign withdrawn and the ad 'I thought the *Kama Sutra* was an Indian restaurant until...' had to be taken down as it turned out that most of the target market really did think the *Kama Sutra* was an Indian restaurant.' Despite, or maybe because of the hassles we took Smirnoff from 300,000 to 2,000,000 cases a year.

"Other marketing high points included a new campaign for Croft Original sherry: 'One instinctively knows when something is right' was the copyline under a dressage horse and rider. Bailey's Irish Cream, Malibu and Archer's Peach Schnapps were launched.

"In 1981 I was promoted to Managing Director IDV Home Trade which was more money but less fun. The authorities had caught up with the

Smirnoff 'Shattering' campaign and we had to tone it down which meant more reliance on the visual and less on the words. Unfortunately they then objected to a girl adrift in a lifebelt holding a Smirnoff Martini. The lifebelt was branded '*SS Titanic*'. If the reprimand from the Advertising Standards Authority was not bad enough, it turned out that the aunt of the then CEO of IDV had perished in that ship. Sense of humour failure prevailed."

Further promotions took Ambler to Group Marketing Director and then joint Group Managing Director but the fun had largely gone and been replaced by endless planning meetings and global travel. 'If I pointed to the errors the companies made around the world, they hated me and if I didn't, I hated myself.' After twenty-eight years, in 1991, it was time for a change.

IDV had been taken over by Grand Metropolitan in1972 and the parent company had been fully supportive. The Chairman, Lord Shepherd, suggested London Business School as a challenging opportunity and was very helpful in securing Ambler's appointment there as a senior fellow, initially to teach international marketing.

Contrary to the many textbooks on this topic, which Ambler claims are 'simply wrong', international marketing is a question of personal relationships, what the Chinese call *guanxi*, not economic analysis. Having discovered that the Chinese got there first (again), he spent time in China amassing the material first for an MBA course at London Business School and then for probably his most successful book *Doing business in China* – both with Morgen Witzel.

His main research successes concerned the measurement of marketing performance and especially brand equity, the asset created by good marketing. 'Return on investment' is the most cited performance measure but, according to Ambler, wholly inappropriate. His book *Marketing and the Bottom Line* remains the definitive text on marketing performance measurement. Neuroscience was explored, the better to understand how marketing and advertising actually work. With the Marketing Society he promoted marketing to non-marketers; with the British Chambers of Commerce he analysed the process of government regulation; and with the Adam Smith Institute he quantified 'taxpayer value' i.e. how better public services could be provided at less public sector cost.

These mostly took the form of monographs, more than twenty in all, and typically thirty page booklets, e.g. *Regulators: Box tickers or burden busters?; Is regulation cause or cure?; Knaves and forks: should we reform Parliament or just blow it up ; EUtopia : What EU would be best and how do we achieve it?* This latter work received high praise from William Hague. In essence the monographs showed

5

the differences between what government said and what they actually did. Regulation is mostly ineffective but promises to cut back on it, at both EU and UK levels, have not been honoured.

He remains a senior fellow of the Adam Smith Institute, the Marketing Society and the Australian Marketing Institute. He was a board member of the Performance Measurement Association and Wolverhampton and Dudley Breweries.

One could regard the eighteen years between leaving IDV and finally leaving London Business School as a long adaptation to retirement. Alternatively Ambler has been too busy to retire. Be that as it may, Ambler accepts that, at seventy-five, it is time to quit. Except he doesn't. His current preoccupation is music composition, mostly for voice, keyboard and wind instruments. At the time of writing he was two- thirds of the way through an Open College of the Arts degree course. Distractions include choral singing, golf and bridge 'all of which follow Oscar Wilde's dictum: if a thing is worth doing, it is worth doing badly.'

Tim's wife Katie has had to put up with all this for over forty-five years. Luckily perhaps her talents lie in different directions, notably art and horticulture. She qualified as a professional picture restorer in London but is now retired from that and painting for herself. They both love opera, well, some opera, but Katie has ballet to herself and her friends.

Gus, their son, is married to Viola, daughter of German academics, and they have two children, Helena and Zachary, aged five and two. They show every sign of being as contrary as their four grandparents.

2.
Richard Worsley

Richard Worsley found it hard to decide on a career. After taking a Cambridge law degree, he thought he might try to become a solicitor but was diverted from his law exams by a broken wrist and other distractions. He next thought seriously about becoming a Benedictine monk – to the horror of his (Roman Catholic) mother, who plotted deviously and in the end successfully to prevent this.

'My mentor for this possibility was the Abbot of Ampleforth, Basil (later Cardinal) Hume. He gave me good and practical advice, and patiently led me to my own decision that the celibate life was not for me.'

After these various false starts, his father, an engineer, decided to take a grip and introduced Richard to the Engineering Employers Federation. This led to his first serious job and fifteen absorbing years in the hurly-burly of industrial relations in the 1960s and 70s.

In 1978 he was headhunted to the CBI, working as Social Affairs Director under John Methven and later Terry Beckett.

'This was a fascinating period, including work behind the scenes on the reform of trade union law, and engaging with the media and the political system for the first time.

'From the CBI I was again head hunted, this time to British Aerospace. After five years, while my bosses were arguing whether to appoint me or someone else to succeed my seriously ill boss as personnel director (for whom I had been deputising for several months), I received another call to move. This time it was to British Telecom where I was to spend fifteen years as personnel director (as it was still called – the ghastly term 'human resources had not yet been invented), covering a very challenging period in transition from nationalisation to privatisation. BT employed 400,000 when I arrived,100,000 by the time I left.

'After some thirty years in huge organisations, and approaching fifty, I started to question whether I wanted that same way of life for another fifteen or so years – and concluded not. I managed to arrange a move to a very different world, running a programme about the 'third age', initially on a generous three-year secondment from BT. The Carnegie Trust had completed an excellent research inquiry on the subject (which BT had helped to fund), and was determined that this should not, like so many similar reports, simply sit on the shelf. I was asked to run a programme campaigning for the recommendations of the inquiry. This involved what was to be a long and eventually successful political battle for age discrimination to be seen as just as important, wasteful and unjust as discrimination on grounds of race or gender.

'This had been an important change for me, and reflected my growing desire to be much more in control of my own work and less at the whim of huge corporations. After six years working for Carnegie, that same thinking led to my last and final career move brought about by the creation of the '*Tomorrow Project*'.

'At the end of the 1970s I had spent a fortnight in Washington DC on a speaking/research trip on behalf of the CBI with one Michael Moynagh. At the end of our visit we found ourselves wondering over lunch in a congenial restaurant what Washington would be like in fifty years time. This led us, over a second bottle, to dream of running a project to debate the answers to that question. Sober reflection and our return to the UK soon persuaded us that it might be unwise to gamble with running a project in Washington, but the seeds had been sown of a futures project and in spare moments in the weeks that followed we laid plans for doing this in the UK. We were much helped by the staff of St George's House in Windsor Castle, who were enthusiastic about basing some of the work there, and we came very near to launching the project in 1980. However, caution prevailed and we decided with some sadness not to throw up our jobs and risk stranding our young families.

'However, fifteen years later, in 1996, when the Carnegie work had reached a natural and reasonably successful conclusion, the circumstances were ripe for pulling out that old file. I tracked down Mike Moynagh, by then a C. of E. clergyman, and we decided to have another go at establishing our' *futures project*'. We embarked on a three-year programme, basing the consultations with experts which were the cornerstone of the work at Windsor. At the end of three years, having published our first report, we had assembled a good network of enthusiasts and supporters, who urged us not to close the project down as planned but to build it into something more permanent. Their enthusiasm was translated into the necessary financial support, and to our amazement the '*Tomorrow Project*' has survived until now. (www.tomorrowproject.net)

'In that period, we have published many reports on the future of work, globalisation, social enterprise, the life course and education. We have established a database of futures trends and still run a programme of events, held at the Royal Society, at which we invite distinguished speakers to offer and debate their views about the future with members of our network of interested individuals, now some 3,500 strong.

'Throughout my time both at Carnegie and in the *Tomorrow Project*, the issue of retirement has been a constant topic for debate. We addressed it in one of our publications, *The Opportunity of a Lifetime*:

'Will there continue to be a sharp break between work and 'retirement'... or might steps be taken to reshape retirement? Might people mix part time work and 'retirement'...might old age be experienced more positively, accelerating a change in how ageing is viewed. We might benefit from the Japanese distinction between being 'old' and being 'aged'. The latter is the more respected condition.

'What we were coming to realise was that in the longterm, retirement as we have known it has no real future. Of course people will want, and need, to slow down, or in some cases to stop working when they get older. But there is something wasteful and illogical about forcing them to do so at a defined age. The diagram below shows, on the lefthand side, a box divided by two horizontal lines, one marking the end of formal education and one marking enforced retirement at either sixty or sixty-five. On top of the retirement line is a retirement period of, on average, fifteen nor twenty years, or in some early retirement cases as much as 30 years.

'The more radical and obvious alternative to the waste of enforced retirement is to stop thinking horizontally. By 2050 our lives are much more likely to be divided vertically, with many transitions between paid work, parenting, learning, unemployment, leisure , voluntary work etc. Instead of inactivity imposed through mandatory retirement, individuals will expect to assemble their own lives, and choose their own transitions. All that employers need is simply to employ people who want to work

From horizontal to vertical lives

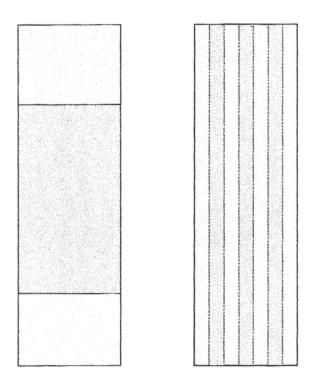

'From horizontal to vertical lives' – Fig 8 from *Opportunity of a Lifetime*

for as long as they meet the needs of the organisation though they have taken some persuasion to accept this.

'Meanwhile, we need to devise new savings systems, rules and incentives which are not founded on the ninetenth century concept of retirement but on the twenty-first century need for lifelong savings to support the various different times of life when we are not earning.

'*The Tomorrow Project*' has been a thoroughly stimulating and enjoyable experience, probably to draw to a close next year. This is not because it has outrun its usefulness; I still think it is hugely important to provide arrangements to encourage people and organisations to think further ahead than comes naturally, and I think and hope we have made some contribution to that.

Richard is seventy next year. There is usually a book on the stocks. He was a contributor to two books about the North Norfolk coast - *The Turn of the Tide* (2005) and *The Return of the Tide* (2010) - writing the conclusion of both and as co-editor of the second. These were collections of essays by distinguished local writers describing the characteristics and vulnerabilities of the 'saltmarsh coast'. A particular pleasure was working with his brother Daniel to produce *I am Horatio Nelson*, a life of the great Norfolk hero to mark the 200th anniversary of Trafalgar.

'This was a fundraising venture (for the Burnham Overy Harbour Trust and to support Sri Lankan victims of the 2004 tsunami). We invited everyone we knew to subscribe to the book (and so get their names on the back). I wrote the first part about Nelson's earlier life, and Daniel took over with his description of the planning, strategy, reality and aftermath of the great battle. The book, written in the imaginary first person, was aimed at children in their teens, but older readers seemed to value it too. A field marshal told us 'well done; you have got the Trafalgar tactics right – and that's not easy.' High praise (for Daniel).'

I am Horatio Nelson raised over £20,000 for the two charities – and is still selling.

Richard's determination to keep his brain going is fulfilled by his current project of translating of Virgil's *Aeneid* from the Latin. He confesses to an obsessive and constant desire to be making something. He is an amateur wood turner and furniture maker, using his father's and grandfather's tools; also an embroiderer (in bargello work). He is teaching himself lettering in wood and would love to learn to make woodcuts and wood engravings. He is also a trustee of two charities one national, one local.

Richard concludes:

'My main feeling about retirement is not to do it. I am certainly not going to retire, though I am reducing the pace. I have seen far too many people thinking of retirement as some sort of cliff edge over which they will have to leap and they are ill-prepared for it when it comes.

'I owe a great debt to Alfred Royer, a friend of my wife's family who taught me about 'recycling'. Every ten years or so, he would sit down in his home in Paris with a blank sheet of paper and set out all the elements of his life work, play, projects, skills, housing, finances, relationships, etc. Then he would mark them out of ten were they satisfying and rewarding, did they make a useful contribution or were they just there because ...they were just there? He would then take a red pencil and cut out the unsatisfactory ones and advise people accordingly. I have done the equivalent twice, and I owe Alfred the credit for some very important decisions about my own life and plans.

'If you are lucky, as I have been, you have the opportunity to change gear from the more intense jobs of earlier years, and aim for things that are equally satisfying, more suited to your own temperament and interests and, above all, more in your own control. But I never want to think about stopping.'

Richard and his wife Stephanie live in a house built for them by Chris Geering, to a design by Nicholas Hills, overlooking the marsh at Burnham Norton. They have three children, all of whom live in London, and five grandchildren.

3.
George Knox

George Knox was born in Tring, Hertfordshire, in 1932. He studied medicine and was called for national service after he qualified as a doctor. He served for three years as a junior medical officer at RAF Marham at a time when the RAF was a very large organisation including five hospitals.

"I had family connections in Norfolk. My mother's first cousin was Rear Admiral Thursfield who lived at Creake Abbey. She asked him if he knew any local doctors who could give good advice and support to this aspiring young man. Dr Woodsend, a local GP, was asked to check me out and flew in his own plane to RAF Marham, dropping out of the sky in dramatic fashion and later taking off again almost vertically.   In the interval between his arrival and departure I had a meeting with him where he did the talking, but he none the less concluded that I was a suitable candidate to become a doctor in the north Norfolk practice.

" There were no patient appointments in those days.   We did all our own dispensing and the practice consisted mainly of home visits. There was just one member of staff who kept the practice organised and achieved an enormous amount of work.   I worked weekends and sometimes three consecutive days and nights without a break.   A GP was very much on his own in those days.   There were just six consultants in King's Lynn compared to eighty-four today.   But the job was just right for me.   I enjoyed visiting my patients, young and old, rich and poor, and continued for twelve happy years during which time Judy and I and our growing family lived in Brancaster.

"Then we moved to Yorkshire to a practice based on Dewsbury.   It was quite different, with a large Muslim community.   We stayed for twenty years.   The community was very family minded.   In the event of a death there was an outpouring of spontaneous grief and it was almost impossible to get near the deceased for the press of mourners. They were kind and appreciative and respectful of one's work.   They were insistent that I accepted gifts to show their appreciation .   These included numerous bottles of aftershave, I wish I could have drunk it, and intriguingly a psychadelic love lamp.   I never did discover what I was supposed to do with that.   In time I became chairman of the Yorkshire postgraduate education   organisation through which hundreds of GP trainees passed over the years.

" For our first twelve years in Dewsbury we lived in a huge Victorian building with high ceilings and windows and *art nouveau* decor.   It belonged to the church and we received much kindness from Bishop Tracey of Wakefield, the former suffragan bishop of Pontefract.   This early mill building had a huge kitchen and had been occupied by the American forces who used linoleum cutouts to simulate carpets.   The building was quite inadequate.   Later we moved to a bungalow with fantastic views over the Pennines and lived there for another eight years.   The terrain in Yorkshire was very demanding particularly in snowy weather.   My hips eventually decided they had had enough of trudging uphill though the snow with my car abandoned at the bottom of the hill unable to negotiate the last half mile.   In 1992 I decided to retire from the rigours of a GP's life and return to Norfolk where I took up a counselling programme teaching young doctors.

" We had bought Cook's Cottage in Overy Town in 1981 and spent the next three years extending it until it could be described in estate agent jargon as 'deceptively spacious'.   I did not look for work but it came steadily none the less.   In 1993 I was appointed clerk of the Wells Quaker Meeting.   I had been attracted by the Quaker ethos for some years.   One of the deciding moments was a home visit to a child patient living at Overy windmill who went to the Quaker school.   I decided that although an Anglican supporter I wanted to become a Quaker.

"In 1994 at the Norwich Quaker Meeting house when nominations were being sought for various positions I was asked if I had any experience in property.   I said I had some experience and they took this on trust.   I was soon to be tested and from 1994 to 1999 I was responsible for surveying and refurbishing some twenty properties in Norfolk to keep them going.   I had been involved in property work in the RAF where medical officers had to make sanitary rounds to assess the conditions in which personnel were living and I gave lectures on building construction pointing out the basics of spotting defects.   I learned for example to detect the causes of rising damp was it a river flowing underneath or did the floor need underpinning...?

"It was suggested by Jane Maufe that I join the League of Friends of Wells hospital and was chairman for many years until the hospital was closed in 2002. I had the privilege of working with Evelyn Rowley,the greatest nurse I have ever met. Harold Macmillan visited the hospital to see a dying friend and was so impressed by the atmosphere that he said this is where he wanted to end his days.   Lord Leicester took on the chairmanship and oversaw the most imaginative programme of bringing new life to the hospital through the installation of the dialysis unit for visitors.   The hospital has now found a successful new role and is getting stronger all the time.

" I was Trustee of the Norfolk Quakers from 1994 to 2008 and have been an Elder of Wells since 2006.   Nothing is forever and Quaker appointments are subject to the triennium rule of three years tenure which focuses the mind even though it is possible to serve for more than one term.   I had three years as chairman of *Wells Churches Together* which is dedicated to ecumenism and encourages tolerance and understanding of doing things together.   We would meet in that most congenial of settings the home of the Bishop of Thetford the fine house in a very English park with its cedar tree, or in the Deanery with its fine furniture facing south.   The Catholics had a centre at ...five miles south of Norwich.   At the millennium in 2000 we had a celebration of Pentecost at Sandringham complete with steam engine belching smoke as custom demanded." George and Judy have been married for fifty-four years and have a large family   There are five children who between them have ten grandchildren.   Classical music is George's hobby and although he owns and plays an electric organ it is strictly for his own amusement.

4.
Pamela Noyes

" I never went to art school, for which I am eternally grateful, thus avoiding a stylised, dyed in the wool approach to painting, regardless of the subject, and preserving the vital sensitivity of expression of the artist's personality.   I have developed the lifelong belief that art is about speaking from the soul.   I feel that I am guided by divine intervention which has helped me battle with self-doubt.

" Painting is a deeply emotional experience . I work at my painting in a shed (studio) in the garden. I can't wait to get down there after seeing to the household needs and my husband Murray, aged eighty –six, who now needs a permanent carer because of his advanced arthritis which has left him almost bedridden.

"I open the door to my shed and a waft of oil paint and turps hits my nose. This must be akin to the experience of actors when they enter their dressing rooms and the smell of greasepaint sets them off on a roll of anticipation and excitement of the challenge of an empty stage, or in my case of an empty canvas. After all these years I still stand, palette knife in hand, before an empty canvas, fearing I will not be any good at painting something stupendous, thrilling and exciting. I suppose what drives me is that 'I want to be noticed'. I need encouragement

Famous artist

to produce my best work and to feel that I matter not just one of the herd to be corralled into submission with the iron gate of authority clanging shut and bolted, allowing only a glimpse *out there* between the bars. I stand expectant, more heroic than I am feeling, in front of a huge oak easel. With a confidence that can only come from long years of experience and scraped off paint, I mix, splodge and smooth my journey through colour, texture and form. Oblivious to everything around me, I struggle through the jungle of emotions all the while hacking and scraping until at last THE THING that I have been waiting for appears. Then I know I must not touch it again. It is the moment all artists work and wait for. The moment when the unbelievable and unspeakable SOMETHING happens.

"Some say you must have a wizard in your life. But where do I find a wizard? Upon a mountain? At the bottom of the sea? On the plains of Africa? NO! say the sages, poking me in the chest. 'Here, you fool in *there'* And they say, 'For God's sake, stay at home; and the wizard will take you anywhere you want to go.'

"I was born in 1929 in Elsing near Dereham. My father the Revd Frederick Arundell Trengrove, the incumbent at the time, had taken this as his first living after his ordination. His wife, my mother, was twenty years younger than him. From what I can remember of those early days we lived in a large and beautiful medieval rectory with its spreading gardens and woodlands with an island in the middle where ducks used to lay their eggs.

"My mother, who gave birth to four daughters – twins, then me, then another girl, all in six years, found the life of a parson's wife in a Norfolk village somewhat daunting. She was beautiful

Pam's mother

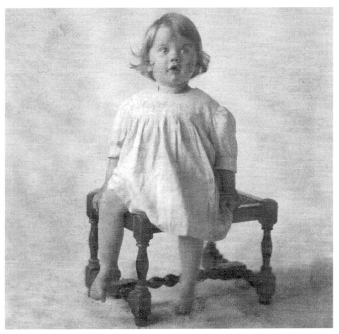

Pam aged two

Haunted rectory

and wild with a sweet temperament. Everyone loved her. She was soft and pliable, generous to the core, giving and easy going and fun to be with. She loved make-up, clothes and going out. The Elsing rectory was reputedly haunted and my father being a Cornishman with possibly a residue of piskie blood was quite intrigued by that phenomenon. He periodically had exorcists in to 'lay the ghosts'. My maternal grandmother, who came to stay quite often, was convinced that she had psychic leanings and swore that one night she saw a 'grey lady' walking along the landing outside her bedroom door and actually heard her long skirts rustling.   When my sisters and I heard her story we shivered at the possibility of meeting this ghostly apparition and from then on I felt the hairs on my neck rise at any talk of ghosts.

"My father was obsessed by them and related Cornish legends to us as we sat around the fire at Christmas I remember them all to this day and they still give me a little shiver. We had various nursemaids living in. One, named Simone, was French, strict and bossy and we didn't like her. We were very pleased when my mother sacked her for not noticing that I was clutching a doll with a broken china head while she washed my hair she thought I was screaming because I didn't like having my hair washed until she noticed there was blood in the washbasin. I had to be taken to the Norwich hospital for stitches and still have a scar under my chin.

"When I was six, my twin sisters eight and the youngest four my father was translated to the joint benefice of Saxlingham and Field Dalling. We lived in the beautiful Georgian rectory at Saxlinghan with its five acres of grounds including woodlands, a tennis court and stables where we eventually kept our ponies and goats. The house was very cold in winter and we squatted around a temperamental fire in what we called the breakfast room. The big rooms were closed up until Easter unless the bishop or some other dignitary came to tea then the drawing room fire would be lit. I suffered badly from chilblains and we only felt warm in summer. None the less we were extremely happy there and we all went to school at Thornage Brecks called Start Point which I loved. I became games captain and took up art and music and benefited from private tutorial. This was the start of my passion for painting and to this day I still feel the urge to slap paint about on large canvasses in mostly impressionist style.

" The repetitive dullness of being a parson's wife with the expectation that she should become an asset to the parish, left my mother more and more bored and frustrated. Her wings were clipped by the endless church services, cleaning altar brass and attending stuffy meetings in a dank village hall among the moustached ladies of the parish clad in grey felt hats and sensible shoes. My father was extremely jealous of her and demanded to know her every movement when she was away from the house. Little wonder she sought solace in an affair with a local landowner which lasted until my father found out about it.

" He was a perplexing mixture of good humour, bad temper and snobbery so I never knew which of these characteristics would emerge at any given time or circumstances.

Sometimes he would laugh at a certain occurrence and at others he would be furious at the same event. The family swayed back and forth on the tides of his emotions. He was rector of Saxlingham and Field Dalling from 1935 to 1961 when he died of heart failure. My mother died in 1963.

"Parents of children at Start Point school were issued with lengths of blue and white floral material to make or have made the uniform summer dresses for their children. My mother, always frugal, made mine herself. The result was a disaster that caused many a titter among my peers - uneven hems, badly set collars, enormous puffed sleeves and sloping shoulders. I hated them and longed for the summer to be over so I would no longer have to compete with the girls from the more affluent families who strutted about in their beautifully cut, professionally finished dresses with buttonholes that actually met the buttons on the front.

"In 1941 the diocesan bishop and his wife were on their annual visit to our house when my mother prepared tea with the best china and aptly named rock cakes. My two older sisters and I had been instructed to appear for a short time during the visit, dressed in our school uniforms which were the only decent clothes we had at the time. As we sat bored and fidgeting the unexpected happened. The bishop's wife caught her elbow on the wing of the armchair spilling her tea all over a cushion. Trying to mop it up with her handkerchief she unearthed a magazine from the depths of the chair. It was a 'Penny Dreadful' presumably introduced by Ella our maid but which my mother had nearly been caught reading when my father appeared and which she had stuffed down the cushions on the chair. The cover revealed a half-naked woman with a man bending lecherously over her. My mother muttered that she must really have a word with Ella."

Pam was just under nineteen when she married Murray Noyes from Burnham Overy Staithe.

" He was in the Navy at the end of the war. We Trennies as we were known did not know anything about Burnham Overy Staithe until one day my father came into the house wielding a sheaf of papers and looking rather excited. He was always looking for new projects. We were having tea at the time with our mother and Ella. His announcement stunned us all. He had bought a convent school complete with PNEU nuns, pupils and staff. It was called St Monica's and he told us he had bought it with a view to some of us eventually going to teacher training college and in future running the school. This was in about 1941, well into the Second World War. We were amazed and it took some time for it to sink in. My mother was quite excited and said she would go a day or two every week to oversee the running of the school. Bored at home she wanted some other interest; we were into our teens and quite independent and could look after ourselves. The school was successful and going well in this lovely village.

" I was very keen on learning the piano and we had a Broadwood Grand in the drawing room on which I was always tinkling. I started having lessons from a pianist from Field Dalling who played the church organ for Sunday services and also at concerts in Norwich. I practised hard in the huge drawing room with no heating of any kind and went on to pass three music exams in Norwich with honours. I played and studied until I got married. We didn't have a piano for many years after that but now I have a Broadwood Boudoir a baby grand, at home and play quite often although my fingers are slightly stiffer. I don't remember a time when I wasn't drawing or painting. As a very young girl I was gap scribbling and making marks on paper when my father, who was very encouraging, bought me my first box of Reeves watercolours which I still have. I used to paint seagulls and terns at Blakeney. When we girls went down on our bikes to swim in the channel at weekends in the summer I found a dead seagull one day and put it in my bicycle basket. On arriving home I propped it up between some books and painted it until it was so smelly I had to throw it out. In summer we would spend long days on the beach and it was there that I first met Murray Noyes whom I was to marry.

"We had two children and lived in a rented farmhouse in Ashwell, Herts. We had a big garden in which Murray built me a shed to paint in. The children were quite small but I managed to fit in some time to paint there and *en plein air* in the surrounding countryside, with a baby on the hip and one running about. They had been born within eleven months of each other.

"Murray was a freelance engineer *par excellence.* He was much sought after for the creativity and perfection of his work; he built boats and houses among other things and was what my friends called a 'car doctor'. One prod and look from him and the car was running again. He was especially keen on Morris Minors. Every screw he used was polished. He had always been a seaman, making his first boat at the early age of ten. Living in Burnham Overy Staithe he taught me to sail and I loved the whole ambience of tides, weather, currents and the sense of being at one with the elements. He had four berth yachts and crab boats with sails that he rigged himself and has sailed most of the seven seas.

"My painting developed well and in 1985 I was accepted for the Summer Exhibition at the Royal Academy. It was a painting of hellebores and when the letter plopped into the hall I could not believe my eyes when

I read it. At the time I was tutoring a group of would- be artists in my studio and when I broke the news to them they jumped about and said 'down to the pub right NOW'. We spent the next couple of hours over gin and tonics and sandwiches . Of course I went to the Varnish Day celebration at the Royal Academy and the lovely service for the artists in a church in Piccadilly.   I met people like Rolf Harris and Diana Armstrong. I also exhibited at the Guildhall in London and at the Malcolm Innes gallery. I am a member of the Cambridge Drawing Society and of the Society of Marine Artists.

"At the age of eighty-three I have no thought of retirement. I have a lot of paintings simmering on the back burner and have every intention of dishing them up for as long as I am allowed.

5.
Chris and Peter Russell

Peter Russell was educated at Wyggeston School, Leicester, where one of his contemporaries was David Attenborough. An assistant scout master at sixteen he went on to read physics at University College Leicester for a batchelor's degree of London University. He then went into the Education Corps for national service directing the science curriculum for sergeants. He was promoted to Captain after six months.

He then went to Loughborough, which became a university, teaching physics and during this time completed a master's degree. He returned to Leicester University as a lecturer and completed his research for his doctorate.

A space research section was created at the university which involved placing a pinhole camera on a Skylark rocket which photographed X-ray activity with long wavelength X-ray technology aimed at the sun.

He became warden of a hall of residence whilst still a part-time lecturer until 1982 when he retired at the age of fifty-five. Peter is now eighty-five so what has he been doing for the last thirty years?

The prospect of retirement is a cause for anxiety for many who see the curtailment of a work-driven, directed life, with its loss of status, as a big void. There is typically regret at a loss of the social interaction of the workplace, anxiety about how to replace it and what to do with oneself. However, this was not a concern for Peter.

"I was very fortunate in that I never worked for a boss or in a system where my hours of work, the days I worked and my holidays were prescribed. The hall of residence had to be managed and led and it was up to me as its warden and my wife Chris, who was integral to its success, how we did it.

"Years later one of the undergraduates who lived in the hall of residence during our wardenship sought out Chris and gave her a letter of thanks for such a memorable time there.

"Chris and I had married in 1949 at Woodmansterne, Surrey, and we moved to Leicester where it was almost impossible to get accommodation so soon after the war."

Chris explained: "We moved into the most basic of flats which was all that was available. It had a cooker that needed black leading and we had to choose between buying a refrigerator and a washing machine. I was teaching home economics at the time and later became deputy head of Evington Hall girl's Grammar school." One of Chris's earlier experiences was in an outer London school.

"There was a 'D' stream class for boys on Friday afternoons. They had spent the morning at woodwork and were hyperactive by the afternoon. Domestic science was seldom their first choice and their behaviour at times left much to be desired however, of this group six went into the Navy as cooks   If someone called for a dishcloth to mop up a spill it would be flung through the air to the boy who wanted it – much quicker than walking.   After more experience in other schools I was lucky to teach at Evington Hall Grammar school and for my last eleven years was deputy head.   When the grammar schools were abolished, or in this case amalgamated with a remote secondary modern school to which there was no dedicated transport, it was time to move on."

Peter continues :
"Chris took on examination work for Oxford University and became chief examiner in needlework and cookery.   I retired from teaching in 1968 but continued my examination work for some years.   We had decided to live in retirement in Burnham Overy Staithe where we had spent many happy holidays over the years.   Furthermore, my family, the Crisps, can trace its history in the area back to 1603 although I wasn't aware of this at the time.   Peter had been Commodore of the sailing club in the late 1960s and was to become Treasurer of the Harbour Trust for thirteen years."

Chris continued: "We bought a holiday cottage in 1968 opposite the entrance to the Moorings Hotel where we used to stay. This was a unique hotel with guests and muddy dogs, wet and cold from sailing, welcomed with all the facilities to dry out and warm up. Whilst we were relaxed about retirement we none the less had no clear plan of what we were going to do when Peter retired in 1982. I had been a magistrate in Leicester for ten years and would have liked to carry on in Norfolk but it was at a time when benches were being scaled down and that was impossible. About this time Peter received an invitation to a Buckingham Palace garden party. The following year, 1968, I received an invitation in my own right so we went twice in consecutive years.

"On arriving in Norfolk I became parish clerk at Burnham Overy parish. Later Peter was elected to the council, eventually taking the chair and was elected on to the parish hall committee. He became involved in the Norfolk Coastal Project which pulled together those groups working in the Area of Outstanding Natural Beauty. The drive behind this was Ross Lambert who involved me initially. At this time Norfolk County Council was encouraging parish councils to start carpet bowling clubs, offering twelve sets at 10 per cent cost. We were keen not to lose the opportunity and offered to pay the £40 to buy one if the parish council didn't wish to take up the offer." As a result of this Peter, with the usual assistance of Chris, became lead organiser for carpet bowls in Norfolk and they organised carpet bowls tournaments throughout the county. They had 360 people at one final in the Sports Village in Norwich."

Chris continues, "We had to find somewhere permanent to live after years on the Leicester campus. Our holiday cottage not being big enough for a main home we had to find something more suitable.

"We found and made an offer for a property in Glebe Lane, Burnham Overy Staithe, but the vendors withdrew it from the market at a very late stage in the hope of getting a better price at auction. We made a new and advantageous offer which was accepted and set about improving the property.

"I set up an embroidery group and ran it for fourteen years. We produced some imaginative, fine-quality church altar frontals for Burnham Westgate and Burnham Norton churches. I derived great joy from working on church embroidery, particularly when I could use gold thread."

Both Chris and Peter are multi-talented. They are both skilled with their hands. Peter made teak furniture and this included a three-piece suite for which Chris made the upholstery. One of Peter's strengths is getting action through people. This led him to the Wells Community Hospital which now has a good model and to the WEA (Workers Educational Association). Chris paints in watercolours preferring their translucency to heavier oil paints. Chris was a Master Bowman and in the 1960s competed with teams from Russia and Poland, winning cups and medals with the English team. It is possible she might have been considered for the Olympic team but work intervened. In those days the bows used were nearer to those of Robin Hood than to the more complicated structures developed today.

They kept Great Dane dogs at one time, the first of which was Hyperion of Ashthorpe, which won the best of breed at Crufts in 1959. Chris tells the story: "We had problems transporting Hyperion to Olympia. Heavy snow meant the proposed car journey had to be abandoned and the train and underground was the only way. He was too big to carry up the escalator. The station master arranged for us to use the lift. Great Danes were bred for boar hunting and travelled inside the coaches whilst Dalmatians ran behind."

Says Peter; "Neither Chris nor I can sit doing nothing and have to keep busy. I suppose I am an unconscious networker and strive to be rigorously efficient. I have long enjoyed chairing meetings which I ensure are well organised. I take the minutes at many of them which makes for an orderly presentation of discussion and action. We have had meetings where there has been a split of opinion on some key issue. It helps to take a straw poll to establish the strength or otherwise for the motion and this tends to close the conflict. Participants at meetings need reminding at times that they have choices. A good chairman will encourage response and pick up on one or more with which he or she agrees and use that to rally the rest and make progress. I have chaired University Convocations where alumni from all universities come together."

Chris started the Burnham Market Ladies' Luncheon Club to run concurrently with Probus meetings which are confined to menfolk. Peter became editor of the *Newsletter* and has continued for many years.

"I took over from the rector who was acting as editor. We had to cut stencils and turn a handle to duplicate the pages. I had the advantage of familiarity with a computer which I brought with me. This was quite novel at the time and it transformed the process and the scope of the publication. Today the *Newsletter* goes to 1300 homes in the Burnhams with a readership of perhaps 5000."

One of the products of Peter's retirement for which the community should be particularly grateful has been his work at the surgery in instigating a patient participation group. This was instrumental in setting up the facility to speak with one's doctor over the phone but in an orderly programme so as not to interrupt consultations. There is a call list at a specific time of the week and the doctor phones the patient. Research shows that there are many more calls on a Monday than for example on a Friday and staffing at the Surgery is planned to meet the fluctuation in demand.

Peter is warm in his praises for the skills and care in the practice. He was suffering from painful stiffness in his joints and asked the doctor to do something for it. He was prescribed some pills and within three weeks on a diminishing dose he felt a new man. Plans to shed some of his workload have possibly gone on hold in his new-found freedom of movement...

6.
Godfrey Sayers

'Although my family roots go deep into the soil of north Norfolk, I was born in Kingston on Thames. My father, a policeman suffered a harrowing time during the London blitz, which resulted in an illness that eventually led to divorce from my mother, who returned home to north Norfolk. As a single parent with two children life was much harder then than it would be now. I, of course, loved it and felt that the war couldn't have been that bad if it had had this result for me, and sixty-five years on I still I know how lucky I was.

' I began my education at Langham then Blakeney primary schools and having missed the opportunity of going to Fakenham grammar school went on to Wells secondary modern.   At Wells I encountered two wonderful teachers who saw some artistic talent hidden under my grubby appearance and mischievous behaviour.   On what was to be an important day for me, my class were invited to paint an important event of the 1950s up to that point; all the class chose the Coronation while I, just to be mischievous, chose the Hungarian revolution and painted a soviet tank with a huge gun pointing at the viewer with a body draped over the barrel.   That painting did it, and between them those teachers arranged for me to have six, sometimes eight periods of art each week, an exceptional occurrence at that time in a Norfolk school.   It was to give me a start and the confidence years later to embark on a career as a painter.   I went on to pass the entrance exams for a place at King's Lynn college where I did well passing all my mock exams with flying colours, and looked to have a rosy future, until fate intervened.

'At that time King's Lynn was a battleground after dark for what were then called 'Teddy Boys' and American servicemen, although if no Americans were around the Teddy Boys had little difficulty finding other victims. Making my way back to my lodgings from college late one evening I became one.   Having worked since the age of nine as a fisherman I was strong and well able to look after myself, as a result one of them was injured.   This news got back to the college principal who had me on the carpet, and while I could genuinely claim to have acted in self-defence, my assertive attitude and non-conforming, self-customised college uniform didn't help my case.   To cut the story short it was my mother not him who decided that I should leave; my being there was stretching her resources to the limit, and should I have managed to get a university place, there was no way I could actually have gone.   People from my background didn't do that; my earnings were needed there and then.

'I left and entered the merchant navy where I stayed for four years; I would certainly have stayed in longer as I loved the life, but I had also fallen in love with my wife. We married when I was twenty-three and I went back to being a mussel fisherman.   In those days there was a large trade in shellfish from north Norfolk to the midlands, Leicester and Nottingham in particular, and I soon realised that the hauliers who came to collect them were making more money than we were.

'So I decided I would do that. I raised a bank loan to buy a five and a half tonne lorry and went on to built up a steady business direct from the quay to the customer, cutting out at least one middleman. This improved freshness and was competitive in price. I negotiated return consignments of shoe manufacturing machinery and materials with the American owned British United Shoe Machinery Co, and because I gave them a same day delivery, I eventually transported all their machinery and materials, plus the post to Norwich and Northampton. I also took on furniture removals to fill in the other days, which led to a very busy schedule. On one occasion I started work at 1.30 a.m. on a Wednesday, completing two trips to the midlands and a large furniture removal that required three trips from Norfolk to Derbyshire, finishing 10.30 on Saturday morning, with no breaks. Part of my attraction to that business was to see the country, as it was in the merchant navy to see the world, however mainland Britain is much smaller and after eight years I felt I had seen as much as you could from the cab of a lorry, also the tight, sometimes almost impossible schedules were beginning to take their toll.

'I had been painting in my spare time for a year or two, mostly very large - astronomical one might say - paintings of the planets of the solar system and other objects in the universe, which had culminated, after an exhibition at the Norwich Theatre Royal, in my illustrating the lecture hall at UEA when the American samples of moon rock toured the country. This along with the confidence those two wonderful teachers had bestowed, furnished me with the courage to turn my last removal vehicle into an art gallery. I put it on the Carnser at Blakeney and instantly became a professional artist; with three young children, that now seems quite mad; I had no amateur career at all. When I see my early work now I wish I'd signed it with someone else's name. The lorry initially cost £1000.00 and I managed 180,000 miles with it on the road and it has been a successful art gallery on the Carnser for thirty- seven years since then. I don't think it owes me anything.

'I was selling pictures locally with some success but only in the summer, in the winter I went back to mussel fishing. But one winter I injured my back which put paid to the fishing work. I was desperate, but as is often the case, fate in the shape of a very dear friend gave me a nudge in the right direction. I would like to believe that all of us at sometime in our lives are lucky enough to have a person who is seminal; someone usually older, who has wisdom and experience, and an opinion you know you can trust, someone who has the belief in you that you may not have yourself. I have been lucky enough to have had three people like that in my life. At this time, it was Margaret Spurrell, a woman of great experience who had known Lillias Rider Haggard, Edward Seago and Henry Williamson and was still friends with Jack Harrison the watercolour painter, who she took me to meet several times and who also encouraged me. Someone like him you believe.

Margaret was certain that there was a market for my work in the London West End stores and suggested I make appointments to see the buyers. I set up a day of appointments, the first was with Liberty's, the one I wanted most because its reputation was unrivalled. I came out of Oxford Street tube too early for my appointment but I went in with my portfolio anyway expecting to wait. The girl in the art department told me that the buyer had already arrived and would see me right away if I wished. He looked through my portfolio and was fairly non-committal but then to my delight and surprise asked if I would be prepared for them put on an exhibition of my work. There had been a cancellation and he wanted me to fill it. It would mean completing seventy paintings and I had just two months to do it. I agreed, cancelled my other appointments in London and returned hot foot to Norfolk with the news. Margaret was so excited, although she said it was no less than she had expected. She was custodian of Lillias's house on the downs above Blakeney, which she offered to me as a base to set up my studio to complete the seventy works. I completed them and the exhibition was a success. I held exhibitions at Liberty's for ten years after that. I then began to paint throughout the year and that was the actual point when I truly became professional. It gave me an income all the year round in place of the earlier seasonal pattern as a just a local artist.

'As I became better known I made a comfortable living and had by the nature of my work the ability to arrange my working hours which gave me the time to become involved in local affairs, that was forty years ago and since that time I have devoted about a quarter of my time and energy to this. The north Norfolk coast is a national treasure to be conserved and protected.

'In 1965 a plan to build over what are now called 'The Pastures' in Blakeney prompted me to found the 'Blakeney Preservation Society'. The group fought this application tooth and nail and pre Area of Outstanding Natural Beauty (AONB) status it was a hard fight to win, but win we did, and today that area-managed by Blakeney Parish Council on behalf of the village is a vital and important open space. It was this victory that gave me the belief that sometimes one person can make a difference.

'Later when I became a parish councillor and after two more battles to prevent development there, we persuaded the local authority to make a compulsory purchase order and the area was acquired for the village in perpetuity.
'Those were exciting years, the implementation of a major tree planting program and the successful dredging of Blakeney Channel for the first time since the 1800s, gave me great satisfaction. I served on the Blakeney parish council for eighteen years and it was the first and happiest of all the challenges of committees and projects.

'It is a difficult admission to make, but I am not naturally subordinate, I like to be in charge of what I do but I can work as part of a team as long as I have some control over where that team goes. I am not happy having to support inferior ideas or being told what to do by people who have not earned their authority.

'The demographics of the area were changing rapidly. Young people were moving away in search of greater opportunities in life and in perfect step their places were taken by an older generation of incomers attracted to a beautiful place to retire. So popular has this coast become that the population doubles in the summer months. Inevitably they brought their own suburban ideas of how the area should be developed and re-organised, resulting in considerable conflict with local residents. At the beginning of this influx and before AONB status was achieved, second home development completely failed to acknowledge or respect the local vernacular and systematically and unwittingly began to homogenise north Norfolk's unique flint cottage villages. Had they set out to work in harmony and with respect for the people and the place they would have received a warmer reception.

'However, there was and is much more going here than the whims of suburbanites wanting coastal retreats. Quangos, like Natural England and EEDA, government legislation, EU Directives and damaging quotas for house building and development have all played a part in homogenising the character of the place.

'Membership of the Blakeney parish council led to me becoming the Central Parishes representative to what was then called the 'Norfolk Coast Project' – now Coast Partnership which is supposed to safeguard the AONB by producing policy guidance for local authorities. The extent to which this failed to do that disappoints me, - Sheringham Shoal wind farm spreads out along the northern horizon directly off Blakeney and there are proposals for more just inland. They failed to object to any of them. But back then it was new and I had high hopes for it.

'At the same time I served as a governor of Edinburgh Road Special school during the difficult and protracted move from Holt to Sheringham. I also became chairman of the National Trust's management committee, later to become BAAG (Blakeney Area Advisory Group) for twenty-two years and more recently I chaired the Norfolk Coast Advisory for the SAC (Special Area of Conservation) for nine years.   I have been chair of Wiveton parish council for the last sixteen years and of the Blakeney Watch House Trust for eighteen years.

'Playing musical chairs on this scale took up a great deal of time, but it was made possible by how I made my living, if I had to be at a meeting in Fakenham at 10.00 am for example, I could (in summer at least) start work in the studio at 5.00 am and get several hours of work in before going.

'I have often wondered what motivated me to do so much, and the only answer I've come up with (beyond social conscience) was that being able to make a living doing something that I loved, and which compared to working as a fisherman was ridiculously easy, made me feel I had to make some recompense for my good fortune. Throughout the years of multiple chairmanships and involvement with the environment I always had it in mind to step back from it when I reached sixty-five. That was the only retirement I would contemplate, simply because I felt that by then I would have earned the right to some time for myself. Retirement from what I do for a living was never an option.

'One day when cycling home from my studio I was reflecting on what my life would be like if I'd had a private income sufficient not to have to work. I imagined a life of leisure, sailing in warm waters and exploring far flung places, both of which I have done anyway, and compared it to my life at that moment. I had just finished a large and quite challenging watercolour. I was putting the finishing touches to a chapter in the book *The Turn of the Tide* and I was also just finishing a web site for my parish council. All of these things had been challenging, but they were also extremely rewarding; each in its own way a culmination of a

Sailing at Blakeney

lifetime's experience and utilisation of all I had taught myself to do.

'Having money and leisure is fine, but a life well lived is about much more than that. To spend our entire working lives acquiring skills, experience and knowledge and to then just stop and throw that all away seems irrational.

'For me there is an enormous difference between doing something because you want to, and doing something because you have to. I have never thought of myself as lacking drive, but the motivation to paint for a living is far greater than just wanting to do it to pass the time, and offers a satisfaction more profound than anything I might find any other way. We are all passing the time here; it's how you do it that matters.

'Keeping pace with times arrow, both mentally and physically, is for me the most important thing. I cycle and swim to keep my body fit and look for mental challenges to exercise my mind; so retirement from the day job was never, and is never, an option. However, letting go of all the other stuff was: I remain Chairman of Wiveton parish council and 'The Blakeney Watch House Trust' but I have let go of all the rest. Occasionally I think that I ought not to have let that experience go to waste either, but then I think it is time for younger people to step up to the plate. The space in my head left from not doing those things I

In Italy

hope to fill with the Italian language, and intend to go to Italy every year from now to see the gardens and renaissance art. I still work as hard as I ever did and for me the only way to spell retirement is' morte.'

42

7.
Steve Benson

Steve Benson,with his commanding presence, deep voice, interest in people, sense of humour and love of acting is an ideal model for a schoolmaster, housemaster and headmaster. And that is exactly what he has been in a career of fifty years. In 1963 this son of an RAF Methodist chaplain, having been awarded a degree from Cambridge and a Dip. Ed. from Oxford saw an advertisement for a history master at Gresham's school in Norfolk. This was familiar territory for his old school, The Leys in Cambridge, played sport against Gresham's. He applied for the job and was interviewed by the then Head, the legendary Logie Bruce-Lockart, and offered the job there and then. Steve as

an all rounder was exactly what Gresham's needed.   He intended to
stay for two years and in fact stayed for eighteen.   He became head
of history and one can only savour the colour and imagination of his
teaching of this, his favourite subject.   After eight years he became a
housemaster and stayed for another ten.

' I arrived at Gresham's in 1964, driving my battered old Volkswagen,
and found myself following another of similar vintage with young
faces looking out of the back window waving.   This I discovered
was the Metson family who lived in Holt.   A week later I was taken
as a lodger into their household.   One of the daughters, Peta, was to
become my wife in 1969.   By 1972 I was head of history and now
became a housemaster.   With the first of our three children we moved
into Woodlands, once a private house which had been extended in 1905
to provide purpose built accommodation for sixty to seventy boys in
the grounds of the school.   I continued coaching games and every
year I produced a house play.   I loved the job and the environment but
after eighteen years I reckoned it was time to move out.   I was forty-
one and wanted to test my suitability to be a Head.   Much had changed
in the educational world and at interview I was faced with new aspects
of education and questions I could not answer.

' I considered it would be a sensible first step to apply for a deputy
headship.   At Bishops Stortford College, a non conformist foundation,
I found what I was looking for.

However after two years the Head retired.   I applied for his job from
within and got it.

There were 350 pupils and 150 juniors.   As Head I missed the teaching
if not the marking.   It is a disadvantage one must accept as a result of
promotion.   None the less I loved the place and stayed there for thirteen
years.   There were difficult times in the 1990s and I opted for early
retirement at fifty-seven.   I had no plan and was 'blissfully undecided'
about what I should do next.   What I did know was that I needed a rest
and to re-organise my life.   We bought a house in Holt, caught up with

many friends we had made there in our Gresham's days and spent time travelling. Then I applied for a job with ISIS East, the Independent Schools Information Service for eastern England, succeeding my good friend Jim Woodhouse. I was appointed to promote the Independent Schools of East Anglia. We did that for example at the Norfolk and Suffolk shows. After five years I retired again.

' In 1997 I was asked to write the history of Gresham's school. This was a joint effort with my colleague the excellent Martin Crossley-Evans. Martin wrote the history from the founding of the school in 1555 by Sir John Gresham. I wrote the history from 1900 when Gresham's was akin to a small grammar school but whose new Head set out to establish it as an education institution with a 'modern curriculum' for a modern age. Classics were put to one side and modern history and geography were introduced together with the sciences for all. The driving force was George Howson, a grammar school boy who did not believe that sport was everything.

'This attracted a new and interesting clientele who were able to shine at Gresham's where they might not have fitted in to a more traditional regime. There was to be no corporal punishment and the boys were put on their honour to keep the three promises they made to their housemaster. There was to be no swearing, no smoking and nothing dishonourable was to be done. The boys were responsible for themselves and if they transgressed they must report themselves to their housemaster. This engendered a very strong feeling of unity. The relationship between staff who did not carry canes and pupils made for a remarkable new school and attracted some otherwise reluctant pupils such as Benjamin Britten, W H Auden, Stephen Spender and numerous children of Liberal MPs. Prefects were given huge responsibilities.

'All good schoolmasters love the limelight. It is a great acting profession. There has been a vibrant dramatic society in Blakeney known as the Blakeney Players for nearly fifty years. They produce two shows a year one in January and the other in July. I was asked to join them in 1998 and continue to be part of the company. We can

45

only rehearse on a Thursday when the hall is available.   The July performance starts work at the end of March and the January show begins rehearsing in October.   We have our own brilliant writers who produce most of our scripts.   My wife, Peta, leads the team painting the scenery.   Others purchase or make the costumes and we have built up a stock housed in two large wooden huts.   Performances are friendly, and closely related to our loyal audience with whom we welcome a measure of interaction.   Young children sit on the floor in front of the rows of chairs for adults.   We have had some memorable productions over the last fifteen years in which I have been involved. I am fortunate to be cast in roles where I sing and have relatively few lines portraying such worthies as an Italian ice-cream vendor, a member of Abba, a spaceship pirate king and Elvis (twice).

'We arrange supper shows on given nights and the proceeds to the Blakeney Twelve team who do valuable community service.'

Steve continues his work caring for and guiding young people.   He is a volunteer panellist for the Norfolk youth offending team giving

his time as a responsible adult to keeping young people – eleven- to seventeen- year- olds - from falling into the criminal court system. Magistrates refer cases to the panel and it plays an important role in assisting them to become responsible members of the community.

Steve has long been a governor in schools including Gresham's, Norwich School, St John's Leatherhead, Ardingly College and The Leys School. 'It's not the committees that attract me but the people on them and the way we can establish an affinity with the Head to help guide the fortunes of the schools.

'Looking back I don't think the prospect of retirement ever pleased me. I was tired and ready to go and fortunate to be able to do so. It seem incredible that that was fifteen years ago. I have no plans to retire as such but recognise that it is time to shed some of the load and reduce the hassle. There is still plenty to keep me reasonably occupied: acting, singing and other local activities. I have never been too keen on gardening and I haven't the temperament for golf or bridge. I love the Norfolk shoreline and the great skies, though I don't scan them with my 'bins' for geese or redshanks. But I'm lucky to live in such a beautiful part of England and to have a wide circle of wonderful friends with whom to wine, dine, laugh and chat. Life is good and I am a lucky fellow. I'm also lazy and have no conscience about whiling away the hours. Retirement to me is a blessing and so long as I have my health, some at least of my memory and the love of family and friends I can see no reason why it should not remain so. I might get involved in a new activity for the next three years or so if it does not call for too much emotional energy. I am aware of what is sensible."

Steve and Peta have two sons one of whom has made his

Grandfather

47

home on a narrow boat, a daughter and four grandsons of whom the eldest is six. He raises money for the church and is a volunteer driver for the Area Caring Society. He is on the committee of Holt Society which aims to promote and protect the Georgian centre of the town.

8.
Peter Christopher Forbes, FCA

With 1948 Olympic torch

"At the age of eighty-three I look back on a varied and sometimes exciting career, and remember that towards the end of my working days I had no real desire to retire. Thus we see a pattern emerge aiming to be involved in something worthwhile, as long as possible. Also it is interesting to see how this aim was almost achieved.

"I was born in Karachi to parents whose whole working life was spent in India after my father's distinguished service in the First World War. He was awarded the DSO for gallantry as a lieutenant aged twenty-six. Our upbringing followed the usual pattern where the children were sent to boarding school in England. However, at the onset of the Second World War all this changed and my brother and I were shipped

49

out to join our parents in India. We sailed out round the Cape, as the Suez Canal was closed. Attended Sheikh Bagh School in Kashmir and returned to England in 1945. At the age of seventeen I went to Clifton College and in the next two years achieved success in sport (1st XV rugby, 1st X1 hockey and school colours for water polo).

" My being undecided on what to do, my mother, a very determined lady, arranged for me to be articled to Turquand Youngs & Co chartered accountants. This was a good move because it provided an invaluable basis for a career in the world of business. My articles were for five years during which time I studied with the aid of a correspondence course and the firm enjoyed my services at minimal cost (£2 per week increased later to £5). On qualification in 1953 the salary offered was £575 a year.

" I decided this was unacceptable so applied to Shell Oil – offer of £1,800 a year but had to go overseas to the West Indies – this struck me as getting the best of both worlds! My territory, as the internal auditor, was Jamaica head office covering Puerto Rico, Panama, Haiti and the Dominican Republic.

" In 1955 I decided to look for pastures new and joined the Hudson's Bay Co. in Canada. Here I encountered a far rougher business environment than in my previous experience and really had to toughen up my approach to survive. My role as controller of the wholesale division, based in Winnipeg, covered 30 wholesale branches stretching from Montreal and Toronto in the east to Vancouver and Victoria in the west, a tea and coffee factory in Vancouver, a liquor division and a garment factory in Winnipeg, including the famous Hudson's Bay blankets.

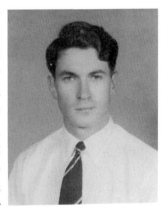

on the eve of departure to West Indies

" After six years in Canada I decided to change direction and, on a holiday trip to England, began to look for opportunities. This led to several job offers, and I considered the two most likely were a potential partnership with Turquand Youngs or at a senior level with a leading management consultancy firm. I weighed up the relative merits in terms of the longterm future and concluded that, despite the more generous offer from the consultancy outfit, Turquand Youngs was probably the quickest route to the top. Hudson's Bay insisted on me working out my notice period of three months and I spent most of this time introducing my successor. One gripe: he started at Can. $12,000 a year and I was on Can. $11,000.

" Joined Turquand Youngs in 1961 as an audit senior, with an over fifty per cent cut in salary. Progressed rapidly to Manager and made Partner on 1st January 1963. Over the years there were a series of mergers and finally the upshot was Ernst & Young, a global accountancy firm, which today is one of the giants of the profession known as the Big Four.

" A great plus in my new life was the greater variety in the work itself and also the opportunity to meet and work with different people, both our own and the clients. Had a long and action packed- career with Ernst & Young and became Lead Partner for a number of multinational companies and also, for the last three years, was in charge of Japanese operations which included trips to Japan.

" My work involved considerable overseas travel and some incidents may amuse: On a flight to New York on *Concorde* – three hours delay before take-off for running repairs. On a voyage to New York on the old *Queen Mary* – dock strike in NY (no tugs or porters) so the ship was placed side on at the end of a wharf and warped round - if went bow first into berth and might have ended up in the middle of Manhattan. Now *Hotel Queen Mary* is moored in concrete in Los Angeles. First trip to Australia: flew direct to Melbourne (took over 20 hours) learnt lesson, all later trips have had a weekend stopover in Hong Kong or Singapore. Trip to Saudi Arabia on a consultancy assignment: had to surrender passport on entry and it was returned at airport on departure.

" In June 1992 came the day for retirement and what to do next? Through various contacts appointed as a director of a private bank and a niche insurance company (insurance and related risk management services for containers and ports worldwide) my main role at these two directorships was as the director responsible for the audit committee. A little later on took up the chairmanship of two pension trustee companies within a quoted company group.

"The insurance company was a leader in its field and the operations spanned the globe. Board meetings took place three times a year: one in each of the main regions: Europe, Asia and the Americas. My involvement in insurance at Ernst & Young stood me in good stead and I greatly enjoyed the opportunity for going abroad three times a year. The board members were a very high-powered group and in the

On a trip to San Fransisco

main were heads of their companies, which were important customers. I remember one interesting case brought to the board for a ruling. A tug was in a South American port and hearing a ship was in distress put out to sea (I understand salvage can be lucrative!). The upshot was the tug sank and the ship was able to continue unaided. The question the board had to debate: was the tug covered for salvage work?

"Alongside the above paid jobs I have had a great deal to do with club committees and a couple of charities. The clubs are the Harlequin Football Club and the Carlton Club. The Quins involvement started as a player in 1948 and over the years, especially after returning from Canada in 1961, was at the centre of things including being honorary secretary for a three year term and in charge of ground development. All changed when the game went professional in 1995. I accept this had to happen but can only say I am pleased that my time was in the amateur days. I am now an Honorary Vice President of the club and not really involved. Next move was to the Carlton Club where I have served on the general committee for three terms of three years and continue to be a member of the house committee.

"Shortly after retiring from Ernst & Young I was invited to become a trustee of the Restoration of Appearance and Function Trust – RAFT. The mission of RAFT is: Restoring Lives through Reconstructive Plastic Surgery Research. When I first joined we had a couple of rooms in Mount Vernon Hospital and later erected a Swedish type building in the hospital grounds. This gave us a fine facility to run the research projects, including access to the burns unit in the hospital, and also room to hold seminars. We held RAFT days to show people round in order to interest and attract donors. The Fire Brigade was a major supporter. The charity now had increased overheads in terms of running costs of the new building, as well as the payroll for researchers and admin personnel.

"Apart from RAFT days various initiatives were taken to attract funds. We held a function in the White Tower in the Tower of London and a concert at the Festival Hall and also less formal occasions. One feature at these less formal occasions was a slide show 'before' and 'after' of patients who had had plastic surgery. Not for the faint-hearted, in fact quite horrendous.

"The other charity I had a role in was set up in answer to the tsunami in Sri Lanka and in particular the coastal village of Kirinda. A group of us got together in Burnham Market to form a team to send out essential equipment to people who had lost everything. This involved having a man on the ground in Sri Lanka, deciding what equipment was needed and sourcing the suppliers in Sri Lanka. A campaign was launched to raise the necessary funds, and proved successful in a relatively short space of time. One of our main concerns was that the equipment should be received by the people it was intended for, and here our man on the ground proved his worth and we received documents and photos showing the recipients. We arranged for distribution of the following: fishing boats, outboard motors, sets of nets, sets of diving equipment, treadle sewing-machines and finally a small computer set-up. The whole exercise lasted for two years and I consider we achieved our goal.

"Casting around for other things to do led me to the Campaign to Protect Rural England - CPRE. I had been a member for many years and, on receiving the notice of an AGM of the west Norfolk district, saw that there was an acting chairman. I attended the meeting and asked about the chairman position – it was made clear that it was not available for me but I was invited to join the committee and did so. My first step, some months later, was to take on being Treasurer and a year or so later, as the acting chairman wished to step down, I was invited to be the Chairman. I have found, and still do, a great deal of interest and perhaps more important a really enjoyable and effective group of people to work with. The latest campaign has been the radical changes to the planning laws and here a measure of success has resulted in significant amendments being made before the final document was issued. Apart from planning matters we organise events for our members – mainly a supper, catered for by members of our committee, an annual lunch and usually one or two other events.

" Among other interests are: Governor of Clifton College, Liveryman of the Worshipful Company of Barbers, Fellow of the Royal Geographical Society, Royal West Norfolk Golf Club and St George's Hill Golf Club.

The Queen's Diamond Jubilee and the London Olympics has made for an event-filled 2012 and I reflect back on what I described as "a varied and sometimes exciting career" – my first retirement was in 1992 and then followed my second career – non-executive directorships and RAFT up to early 2005.

" Since then and today the future is still full of interest: CPRE / Carlton Club / Norfolk Club / Last year renewed my debenture seats at Twickenham for a further ten years / Chairman of the Tenants' Association of a block of flats in London / the committee of the Burnhams Society.

"The best move I ever made was to marry Jane, who has been my loyal companion, guide and inspiration through thick and thin. With her I now enjoy our home in Burnham Market, our beloved dog Cindy and our interest in the grandchildren and their exciting activities."

With Cindy

9.
Trevor and Christine Forecast

Trevor and Christine are a great team. For the last thirty years they have worked together on some seriously impressive achievements in the hotel and tourism industry. They met when Trevor, who in his spare time ran a dance band, was asked to play at Christine's twenty-first birthday party in 1961. Both were pursuing successful careers when they married in 1963.

Christine takes up the story:

"I was an occupational therapist at the Shenley Psychiatric hospital. There were 2300 patients and the objective was to enable as many as possible to return to a normal life in the community, recognising that many were from disturbed families. Later I moved to the Queen Elizabeth Hospital in Welwyn Garden City, the first general hospital to open with a psychiatric unit attached.

"I ran an industrial unit sorting stamps into display packs, packaging Goya and other products, making metalwork objects with the tools of the trade which included a brazing torch. The job was not without its dangers as some patients could be unpredictable. I also ran a typing pool for short-term patients so they could keep up their speeds and shorthand skills. I found great satisfaction in the work and the sense of achievement seeing patients progress."

Trevor became a chartered engineer after completing a five year engineering apprenticeship with De Havilland Aircraft. After national service he moved on to become Marketing Manager for the Polymer Corporation UK, working on projects using engineering plastics to replace metal bearings and to cut the noise and smooth the transit of metal products in manufacturing. After fourteen years the company announced that there were openings in Germany and Australia. Trevor was aged thirty eight and had always aimed to run his own show by the age of forty. It was time to make a decision on a career move which would enable Christine and him to work more closely with people. He and Christine, who was raising a young family at the time, focused on owning and running a hotel, preferably out of town with a country house ambience.

"We trawled the advertised hotels for sale and after a year in which we looked at ninety decided to take some good advice and find our first hotel in a town. This had the advantage that our guests were transient and we could learn our business from throughput. Later we were able to apply this expertise to a unique hotel destination where regular customers found the qualities they sought. These were senior businessmen, visitors to local companies and tourists who wanted something better than the run-of- the- mill and individual attention.

"Our first venture was the Crown Hotel at Downham Market which we owned and ran from 1972 until 1982. We immediately became involved in encouraging tourism to west Norfolk, introduced the first Downham Market Trades Fair and Festival Week with over 1000 people through the courtyard of the Crown. In 1982 our dream came true and we bought Congham Hall. This fine, attractive building had been a private house and we determined to

Congham Hall

retain as much of this ambience as possible. It needed substantial renovation to recreate the feel of an elegant country house. Christine planted a large herb garden at a time when herbs were coming into fashion and this was publicised throughout Norfolk, the UK and internationally prompting visits from the herb societies of Germany, Japan and the USA.

The herb garden

Trevor was invited to start the King's Lynn Hotel and Catering Association in 1984 and for three years he worked with the Council to develop Tourism in west Norfolk and encouraging schools careers festivals. This led to other key appointments on the Borough Council tourism committees. He

59

still represents the British Hospitality Association on their eastern regional committee and the King's Lynn Hospitality Association.

Trevor was sixty-five in 1999 when they sold Congham Hall after a long struggle to obtain planning permission to enable them to extend its facilities and take it into a different league.

They had no real wish to retire but with more staff to run a larger hotel they would have been able to delegate responsibilities and still enjoy being involved in developing their passion. However, following their decision to sell they started plans to open a boutique-styled bed and breakfast in a town or nearby city but the serious illness of their son-in-law Paul made this impossible. He was a very successful contract caterer who had trained at the Savoy and the Ritz. At the age of thirty he had a seizure whilst driving from Welwyn Garden City to London. He survived the car crash but was diagnosed with a brain tumour. He was told that he would live for the five months until their second child was born and, as his tumour was a slow-growing astrocytoma, which had grown from his childhood, he was able to work on for two years but died afterfive very traumatic years. Family came first for Trevor and Christine. After Paul was diagnosed they gave up all thought of pursuing the bed and breakfast venture.

Their elder daughter Katie, a nutritional therapist, started the Astro Fund charity in 2001 to be a point of contact, to collect money and source information on care and lifestyle for the sufferers of the condition astroglioma from which Paul died. Katie organises the research and Christine is the secretary and, together with other trustees and supporters, they work tirelessly arranging fundraising events and publicising the existence of slow-growing brain tumours. More children and those under forty die from a brain tumour than from any other type of cancer but less than one per cent of the total cancer funding in the UK goes to brain cancer research. Paediatric low- grade gliomas are the most common tumours of the central nervous system in children, accounting for almost fifty per cent of all childhood brain tumours.

The Astro Fund has over 300 people worldwide supporting each other on their online support groups. They consist of patients, carers, friends and family members around the globe who can expand upon all the information available from the charity's website. The mission of Astro Fund is to fund low-grade glioma (LGG) research, and to provide a focus for the low-grade community by offering a source of information, inspiration, connections and hope.

Katie Sheen has very talented children. Her eldest son Jack is a composer of classical music and at the age of eighteen was BBC 2011 young composer of the year. He composed for the National Youth Orchestra and was commissioned to write a five minute work for the Royal Philharmonic Orchestra. His specialism is string instruments but he has also qualified at grade 8 piano. His younger brother Freddie is in the under nineteen England lacrosse squad. He is also an excellent hobby chef but despite the alternative career this might offer has chosen engineering.

Paul's widow Emma, their younger daughter, lives in Holt and has a boy and a girl both of whom go to Gresham's school where they are very happy.

So retirement has always been busy for Christine and Trevor.

"In one way it was very easy for us to adjust because, working together for over thirty-five years we were used to seeing each other all day; some couples seem to find this quite difficult. On the other hand we were used to working in the evenings at the hotel and found quiet evenings with nothing to do quite difficult to adjust to. How people sit and watch TV all evening I really don't know. We both feel that the secret of successful retirement is to keep busy on the things that really interest you."

Trevor has pursued his interests in hotel and tourism related organisations. He continues on the regional committee of the British Hospitality Association and was Chairman of the Master Innholders of Great Britain in the year 2000 & is still an active member. This exclusive organisation includes the most professional and dedicated hoteliers in the land and is a development from the Innholder's Livery Company to ensure the continuity, training & connection with the profession of being an 'Innholder'.

He has a long association with the Duke of Edinburgh's Award and, upon retirement was invited to be Chairman of the West Norfolk Award Scheme for ten years from 2000. He is still on the fundraising committee for them

and keeps up his contacts. They live in Sedgeford where there is jolly social crowd – there always is when Trevor and Christine are around.

He has had a lifelong interest as a member of the MG car club and he and Christine enjoy rallies around Britain, not least the autumn tour where some sixty MGs take part, and indulge their interest in attractive hotels and pubs. They have toured Belgium and France.

Trevor has a lifelong interest in rugby which he played with his fellow old boys of St Albans School until the age of thirty-four. He started a rugby club in Downham Market in 1974 which lasted for twenty-five years.

"We are never bored," says Trevor, "every day is an adventure to be savoured" He and Christine go to pilates every week, visit their favourite restaurants and friends between walks on the beach and keep as fit as the years allow. They are amusing and good company. Both are people persons and throughout their career they have had an affinity for young people to be encouraged in their work and qualifications. Trevor worked closely with the College of West Anglia in King's Lynn and the Norwich City College Hotel School, lecturing in marketing and careers in the industry. That interest continued well beyond retirement age.

10
Peggy Sizeland

Peggy was born in Stiffkey at the home of her grandmother. When ten days old she came home to the family cottage opposite Jimmy Riches shop in Burnham Overy Staithe. He was a well-known character and ran the shop for sixty years. His wife worked in the shop and when she wasn't looking he would slip us children a sweet or two. He was known as 'Daddy Riches'.

Her father, Jack Bickell, was a builder on a large scale employing forty men. By 1970, aged thirteen, she was assisting the Revd and Mrs Moore at Sunday school at Burnham Overy Town. Peggy is a very caring person and has been involved in helping the community all her life.

"We did not own much as children but appreciated and shared what we had. We did not want because we had and appreciated what we needed. This included my best coat made out of a grey army blanket. I shared this with my four best friends to go to parties and we shared dolls and clothes made by my auntie, May Sandell. We searched for pieces of coal by the sea and would co-operate near Sally Thompson's shop to find orange wrappers which could be cut in to strips for toilet paper. We were alert to the windfalls that were occasionally washed up on the beach. A ship carrying lard foundered off the coast and many residents turned out with a range of containers to cut off lumps of it. There was another ship carrying grapefruit which came to grief. Today children have a whole list of wants which have little to do with what they need. Parents will buy presents to pacify tantrums and submit to being pestered by their children who want to keep up with the trends set by their friends. Respect for possessions has declined as easy-come gifts have increased.

"The east coast floods in 1953 were the most terrifying experience I can remember. I was aged thirteen at the time There was no warning of what was to come although it was very windy. The waters were suddenly upon us and, with no mobile phones in those days, word was slow alerting residents down the coast. I was in Hunstanton on my own at a friend's house when I heard of drowning and I was desperate to get home thinking that my mum and dad would not be at home any more.

" We had long been associated with the sea. On my dad's side we were related to Johnny Bean who later ran seal boats out of Morston to Blakeney Point. Both he and Joe Read, warden of Blakeney Point, were married to my cousins.

" When my dad was on active service we had some structural problems to sort out in the cottage in Burnham Overy and the staircase was in a poor state of repair. My father asked builder Welcome Thompson to replace it. He removed the old staircase but did not know how to build a new one and so he installed a ladder for us to climb to the first floor. This went on for months until my father returned and insisted on a new staircase. Another member of the Thompson family, Sally, produced ice cream which was nearer to custard and promoted it in the neighbourhood as 'approved by the medical profession'. In fact the local doctor was an enthusiast for it and he was the medical profession referred to. It was the best. We would collect jam jars and take them for the deposit to Jimmy Riches for a farthing. Then we would go and buy ice cream."

Peggy and Harry got married in 1960 and lived in a cottage behind the Hoste in Burnham Market for nineteen years, then to Burnham Overy Town for eleven years and then back to Burnham Overy Staithe. Harry was in the building trade with Jack. Peggy and Harry have three sons. Tim has his own painting and decorating business, Mark and Paul have their own building firm with grandson Richard, called Norfolk Coast. They also have two daughters- in- law, Louise and Primrose and three grandchildren, Richard, Christopher and Chloe, who are a very big part of their lives.

Once the boys were old enough Peggy determined to go out to work. The building trade was very difficult in the 1970s and having decided on a career in caring and nursing she became a night nurse at Westgate Hall in 1981. She did an initial nursing course at Lynn College and so many hours at the Queen Elizabeth Hospital. Westgate Hall had forty-two elderly residents and it was usual to be checked by the police for suitability before starting such work. This was in 1981. " However I received an urgent call to start work at once and 'policing' did not happen until three months later by which time I was well established in my job. I did three years of night duty and then became a relief officer until Westgate Hall shut in 1990. Part of my duties was to go on a bereavement course located at the George Hotel, Swaffham. On my days off I also helped the Forget- Me- Not Club as a driver on some outings.

" When my father died Harry and my mother took over running the building business until they retired. Harry and I have been married for fifty-two years. He never misses a football match and played until he was forty-two. He is now a very loyal spectator. I did not go to football matches as it gave me time on my own.

"I worked for Social Services for twenty years with no thought of retiring. But I had an accident on the ice and the snow. I slipped and my leg shot out from under me sustaining serious damage. After an agonising period of six months during which the specialist drilled a hole through my knee and washed it out to remove bits of broken cartilage, he advised me to retire and I had to come to that reluctant conclusion. At fifty-nine this came as a shock. My work had been my life and I love people. The prospect of being at home all day filled my life with dread. Harry, who is eight years older, had already retired. After seven months I wanted to get back into my uniform and resume my work.

" Then my old headmistress needed caring for, and I was asked to look after her. This lasted for seventeen months. There followed the worst three years of my life. My mother was killed in a car accident, my sister died of cancer at fifty-two and a cousin died some twenty weeks later from a heart attack, also fifty-two. The motorist involved in my mother's death was brought to trial and we failed in our efforts to keep him out of prison. The police were very helpful and we wanted to return their kindness over the court case.

" I had been elected to the parish council in 1999 and served for twelve years. I became vice- chair and volunteered for the Local Action Group (LAG), working in close co-operation with the police and other agencies. LAG became SNAP. We encouraged community action and among the most popular were skate parks which give young people something enjoyable to do.

"I developed cancer of the colon in 2007. My first indication that something was wrong was when my daughter- in- law's boxer dog kept nuzzling my stomach and I could not understand why. I went to a spiritual healer but she said I should go and see my doctor which I did. The condition was very advanced and I had an operation in the Queen Elizabeth Hospital. After intensive care I went home and the district nurses were outstanding as were my family and friends. I had seven months of chemotherapy while I picked up my life.

" I looked for activity that I could carry on at home and started knitting bonnets for premature babies. We have formed a circle to help meet the demand of 500 bonnets a month at the Queen Elizabeth Hospital. There are five of us at work and the champion knitter has produced 300. If I really work at it I can knit three in an evening using whatever wool is available.

"In 2010 at the age of sixty-nine I started the Burnham Market Youth Club which meets weekly. Wednesday evenings are for seven-to-ten-year-olds and Thursday evenings for eleven-to-seventeen-year-olds. It has been very successful with all the volunteers and I really enjoy helping young people. I sell secondhand books to help raise funds for the youth club. I have also tried to encourage affordable housing in Burnham Overy since 2000 but this has proved to be an endless battle against prejudice.

" I have never fully got over my early forced retirement. I cannot sit and watch television in the day. I must be doing something. I keep in touch with friends I have known for years but as we get older the number inevitably dwindles and one loses touch with others. I just wish my sister Marion was a bit closer.

Recently I have joined the committee of the Burnhams Society. This is dedicated to conserving and enhancing the environment of all the Burnhams. We support projects in co-operation with the parish councils. I look forward to identifying opportunities to support the community. I am a member of the ladies' British Legion.

And retirement?..not while I still have the health, strength and my family.

11
Pam Swinburn

Pam was under no pressure from her parents to take any particular career path and chose scientific subjects at school and university. She took a job in the Lyons laboratories as Margaret Thatcher was to do before she became a politician. Pam married Desmond in 1952. They had met in 1945 in the choir at the youth club run by the John Keble church in Mill Hill when Pam was still at school. Desmond was the sub- organist at Peterborough cathedral and their courtship carried on when Pam went to Exeter University. He was a music teacher and organist and they lived in Richmond, Yorkshire, for five years. Pam beat five men to a job with the Wear Tees river board and became a champion of women's rights, interested rather than militant. One of her early successes was to fight for a loo for the ladies!

" We have three children – girl, boy, girl - and moved around the country as Desmond secured better teaching and musical posts. Moving from Yorkshire to Surrey, first to Sutton and thence to Dorking, and finally to Beverley in east Yorkshire. We first discovered Burnham Market in 1959 and decided that we would finally hope to retire there. For our holidays in and around Burnham Overy Staithe we first camped in the best Girl Guide tradition. (Wherever I lived I became very involved in the Girl Guide movement.)

"We quickly decided that a boat was imperative and took up sailing with great enthusiasm. We had a variety of small boats including a Tideway and as the children became keen sailors we also had a Merlin Rocket which was much faster, later discovering that we were known as the 'Merliners' by the sailing fraternity. For five years we rented houses in Burnham Market and then for the next twenty years we owned a cottage in South Creake.

"Dorking in the early sixties was a remarkably coherent community some twenty-four miles south of Central London. Many people in the town came together for music making inspired by the Leith Hill festival founded by Vaughn Williams who lived there. Desmond was much involved in these activities and we frequently entertained the soloists when they performed in the town. Whilst living there I was a founder member of the Evening Townswomen's Guild and later became a member of the mid Surrey federation. I also represented the Townswomen's Guild in a television broadcast and in a radio interview, discussing the pros and cons of being a chairman (no chairperson in those days!). On the federation committee my special interests were public affairs and drama and I chaired both the sub- committees. Also in Dorking I became a swimming teacher for Surrey County Council and found it most rewarding to see a class of small children gaining confidence in the water and learning to swim.

"I found that I was happiest when with people, and when we moved to Beverley I again became involved with the Townswomens Guild, finishing as chairman of the East Yorkshire federation. People's attitudes were rather different from what I had been used to and when I offered to give friends a lift to a meeting I was asked, 'Won't you have to get home to get your husband's tea?'

"I also decided that I needed to do something creative so I went to classes to learn how to make Japanese silk ribbon flowers, a skill which stood me in good stead when I moved to Burnham Market where I demonstrated to Women's Institutes and at the County Show in Norwich and at Sandringham. I also had a stall at Burnham Market Craft Fair for two years. This had to meet Anne Cringle's exacting standards.

"Beverley and Hull were quite a culture shock after living in commuter Surrey for twenty years. However, because Desmond was organist of the City Church in Hull we both joined the Hull Civic Society. Living in a listed Georgian house we became interested in buildings and I became a town guide and member of the Civic Society committee. We also became founder members of the National Trust Association in east Yorkshire and held numerous fund raising events in our house. For many years I delivered meals on wheels.

"I decided that I needed to fill my days so became a self-employed market researcher, working for MORI and numerous other companies. The work was varied and frequently very interesting especially when interviewing executives of companies with either a case of wine or whisky in the boot of my car. House- to- house interviewing could be quite scary, very amusing or absolutely fascinating. One rather elderly lady, on being asked whether she used deodorants claimed that she used Domestos for everything. This was on the doorstep with several neighbours listening in.

"I made it a firm rule never to accept a drink in someone's house. However, I met one delightful couple both 100 years old, in an immaculate house and who kept me spellbound telling about the very hard life they had had on Humber keel boats. Needless to say I enjoyed a cup of tea with them. One man was so annoyed that his wife had agreed to be interviewed that he locked me in the house until

71

I tore up the interview. My *bete noir* however, was aggressive dogs or being asked from a window if I was the 'social'.

"Do researchers believe what they are told? You get a feeling about whether or not you are being told the truth. If as an interviewer you are older and on your own, the chances are that people are more willing to be interviewed. It is fatal to be accompanied by another person. This causes reticence, suspicion, or showing off. On the whole, election canvassing proved to be accurate. I canvassed for MORI the night before an election and the result was very similar to the canvass. It was most satisfying to phone in your results before six o'clock in the evening and hear the outcome of the survey on the ten o'clock news. It was none the less reassuring that Desmond was occasionally sitting in the car outside when visiting houses in some of the rougher estates in Hull at night.

"When Desmond retired in 1986 we moved to Burnham Market into Galen House with its large and beautifully kept garden, the scene of open gardens and many a fundraising function. Our focus in Burnham Market moved to Westgate church initially. Within two months we had both been co-opted on to the PCC of the church. I also joined the WI and once again became involved in drama.

"I volunteered to do house- to- house collections for various charities and found this an excellent way to get to know people. Through the enthusiasm of Peter Russell I was soon co-opted on to the committee of the Workers Education Association (WEA). This led to my becoming a member of the Norfolk federation, its chairman and a member of the summer schools sub- committee. For several years I was chairman of the village hall committee and founder member of the carpet bowls club, a popular competitive pastime across Norfolk. Once again I became involved in delivering meals on wheels, sometimes having to wash the plates before putting food on them.

"The Friends of St Mary's Burnham Westgate was formed when four large holes appeared in the aisles and it became apparent that we would need to raise a large sum of money. To my consternation I was elected

Secretary in my absence.   Initially we organised a money- raising event every month and had a very enthusiastic chairman.   The long-established organist at St Mary's was Joyce Farrow and when she decided to retire Desmond was offered the job.   This roughly coincided with the formation of the Friends and Desmond organised several concerts with choir and orchestra which filled the church and raised a considerable amount of money.   He also ran a W I choir and wrote the music and played for several W I pantomimes.   His choir, the Burnhams Singers, also sang at many carol services in Westgate church.

"We both had a strong bond with Lady Margaret Douglas-Home whose influence and energy did so much for the village including the Craft Fair and the annual art exhibition in St Mary's church with which we were much involved.

"Despite the fact that we are both into our eighties we none the less sought pastures new in 2010 and moved to a charming period house in King's Lynn.   This is one of many merchants' houses dating back to

Diamond wedding

about 1740 in the old and thankfully unspoiled part of the town. One great advantage of this is being able to exchange almost one acre of garden for a small but very attractive courtyard garden. I still keep in touch with the WEA both locally and with the Norfolk federation but enjoy being able to go to numerous talks and lectures without having to be involved in their planning. King's Lynn has a strong sense of the history of its Hanseatic past and also a very active Civic Society of which we are members.

Des at the organ at home

"We celebrated our Diamond Wedding in 2012 and the Queen's Chapel of the Savoy, where Desmond trained the boys in the choir twenty years ago put on a special service for us in May. It has indeed been a vintage year for diamond weddings. In all my various activities Desmond has always been there to offer help and advice.

Pam's outlook on life can probably be summed up in 6 words:

Can I do anything to help?

12
Rosalie Monbiot OBE

It must be a record. Rosalie Monbiot OBE has been actively involved as a school governor for forty-seven years and is still Chairman of three local school governing bodies. She has been involved with over thirty charities in the last thirty years and a councillor for thirty-one years. Her service to the community started as soon as she left the London School of Economics and became a hospital almoner at Hackney Hospital. Service to the community was a feature of her family. Her father was Roger Gresham Cooke CBE MP and her mother Anne, daughter of Hugh Pinckney CBE, was tireless as a JP and an MP's wife.

Born in Hungerford, Berkshire, Rosalie was educated at home and then the PNEU school at Overstone, Northampton.

"My father was Secretary of United Steel in Sheffield during the war and we lived in Yorkshire – a long way from boarding school in Northampton when petrol was scarce. My parents took me to school at the beginning of term and I seldom saw them or my three siblings in term time. I then went on to a scholarship at Smith College, Massachusetts, USA – a marvellous year – and returned to LSE. I joined the Young Conservatives. It was either that or the Young Farmers in those days and living in London the latter was not an option. I was a secretary to Harold Macmillan on his 1959 election tour.

" In 1960 I met Raymond Monbiot, my husband to be, a fellow YC who was a sales manager with Lyons. I was planning to go to Hong Kong for a year as a secretary to Butterfield and Swire and our understanding was that if we still felt the same about each other when I returned we would get engaged. In my absence my father, a keen yachtsman, initiated Raymond for the first time into sailing and when out of sight of land asked him what his intentions were towards his daughter. No pressure! I returned from Hong Kong and we got engaged after an unexpected win at bridge against my grandparents. We had been out together that day to Swindon and the Uffington White Horse on the Downs. The combined experience had its effect. We got engaged and my mother looked forward to a quiet country wedding in Hungerford. However, my father had other ideas and invited most of the Parliamentary party to our wedding in St Margaret's, Westminster with the reception in the House of Commons. Canon Michael Stancliffe married us and later christened George in the Crypt of the House of Commons of which he was Chaplain. We honeymooned at the Mamounia Hotel in Marrakesh, Morocco.

"We lived near Rickmansworth for four years until we found a house in the village of Peppard Common outside Henley- on- Thames where we lived for thirty-five years."

It was here that Rosalie established roots in the local community becoming chairman of the parish council, a member of the Henley Rural District Council and subsequently South Oxfordshire District

Council of which she became Leader. She served on the local health authority and was its Vice Chairman before becoming Chairman of the Royal Berks Ambulance Service Trust. This was a position she loved as the dedication of the staff to their patients was paramount. At the same time she was Chairman of the Oxfordshire Scout Association – the only female chairman in the country at the time - and the Board of Visitors of Huntercombe Young Offenders Institution which was a fascinating insight into the minds of young men.

"My experience extended to housing associations, Children's Aid Direct international charity, the Henley Youth Centre,where I arranged a visit from HM The Queen in 1998, the National Autistic Society and I was a ministerial nominee as a member of the Southern Council for Sport and Recreation."

In 1992 Rosalie was awarded the OBE for her services to the community. By this time she and Raymond had three children. George, a dedicated and visionary environmentalist who writes for the Guardian. Katherine who died of anorexia at the age of thirty-one and Eleanor who

George

lives in Kenya with her former regular a r m y h u s b a n d in a house they built themselves surrounded by the open bush with 150 different species of wild animals and birds. She is a director of World Vision, travels the world and was awarded the OBE at the age of thirty-four.

Granddaughter Hanna

Katherine   Eleanor

In 2000 Rosalie and Raymond moved house to Norfolk. Rosalie's family had owned The Friary at Blakeney for 100 years and it was the preferred holiday destination. Raymond was chairman of Campbells Soups in King's Lynn for six years so Norfolk was familiar territory. None the less they were advised that it would take twenty-five years before being assimilated into the community. As it happened it took one week. The former Personnel Director of Campbells had arranged an invitation to join the celebration of Peggy Davies' 80th birthday. Half the village was there and by the time the party ended they had joined the Friends of St Mary's Church, the Gardening Club, the Burnham Market Society and agreed to help with the teas at the Norton church fete. They recall being welcomed with enthusiasm, not least because 'It was nice to see younger people!' They were both in their middle 60s.

Rosalie had come to Norfolk to retire but six days after moving in she was approached to stand for the county council. She served on it for eight years and became the Cabinet member for Childrens' Services, a job from which she derived huge satisfaction as it covered both education and social care of young people.

" I have maintained and developed my interests in school governorships in Norfolk," she says, " extending my involvement to different schools and age ranges. For example I am Chairman of Redgate junior school and Hunstanton infant school and Burnham Market primary school. I am a member of the Diocesan Board of Education and a Governor of Gresham's school, Holt.

"One of the most demanding roles I have undertaken is as a member of the Burnham Market parish council. Where a county councillor has a big task in a wide territory and covers a large portfolio such as Children's Services, the parish council is closer to the people who share life in the village. One's involvement is more immediate and relevant to the daily lives of its residents. Moreover Burnham Market has seventy-three per cent second homes and the fluctuation between the crowds in the summer and the relative quiet of the winter is significant. There are fewer residents each year who will take on community roles. The volunteer population is ageing and the work of keeping the village functioning does not abate.

"I derive a great deal of pleasure from attracting and feeding the birds who come to the garden. We have a large number of goldfinches.

With Boris

Partridges and pheasants visit us attracted by the safe atmosphere. Our cat Boris catches mice and small rabbits, proudly presenting these dead or alive over night for our inspection but he never touches the birds and they have a mutual rapport. We have a goose we call Lucy

Bubbles with Lucy

who flew in to take up residence on our pond. She is a white farmyard goose who seems to think she is a horse, an inseparable companion who is to be found around the feet of the horses grazing our fields. At dusk I call to the hedgehogs to come for their supper. Our favourite is called Peanut reflecting his diet of peanut butter and hedgehog mix.

Peanut

If we fed him catfood it would be eaten by Boris who is already a huge cat. He moved in with us after the two we brought with us from Henley died. Since we have encouraged the hedgehogs we have had very little slug activity. I also enjoy going racing at Fakenham which has such an intimate and friendly atmosphere.

Golden wedding breakfast in the Kenya bush

81

In 2011 we celebrated our Golden Wedding with lunch parties for 100 good friends. A highlight of the celebrations was our visit to Kenya and a breakfast in the bush.

13
John Bell

John Bell, the youngest of four surviving children, was born in Doncaster in 1935. His father came originally from Lancashire, though his antecedents had come from the Yorkshire Dales around Richmond. His mother, also from farming stock in the lower Dales, died when he was four years old. There was a harmonious fusion of Lancashire and Yorkshire in his ancestry which he has traced back to the mid-eighteenth century so far.

After school in Yorkshire, where he took the last of the old School Certificates in 1950, John joined *HMS Conway* prior to his entry into the Merchant Navy in 1952. *HMS Conway* was originally built as *HMS Nile* in 1834, a wooden 94-gun battleship of the line and had been moored off Rock Ferry in the Mersey since the 1870s as a training ship for Royal and Merchant Navy Officers. The threat from German incendiaries prompted her transfer to the Menai Straits in 1941. Tragically she was lost in 1953 when, whilst being towed back to Liverpool for dry-docking and a refit, a forward towline parted during the passage through the treacherous waters between the tubular and suspension bridges connecting Anglesey to the mainland (an area known as the Swellies) resulting in her grounding and breaking her back on the rocky Caernarvon shore.

For the next ten years he worked for Port Line (now defunct like the rest of the British Merchant Navy) a subsidiary of Cunard, which operated thirty-four refrigerated cargo passenger liners from European ports to and from New Zealand and Australia via South Africa and/or the Suez and Panama canals. He was originally indentured as an apprentice, his father having paid a premium of £30 to guarantee his good behaviour, and was paid the princely sum of £10 per month for which, amongst other things, he undertook not to 'frequent taverns or alehouses nor play at unlawful games'. He eventually achieved the rank of second navigating officer but left the sea in 1961 following his marriage to Anne in 1960. He retained his love of the sea, and has sailed extensively around the English Channel, northern Biscay, the Irish Sea, west coast of Scotland and the Mediterranean up to the present day holding an offshore yachtmaster's certificate. For many years he took a party of friends (the common denominator was agriculture or rugby) on an annual cruise. They called themselves the ' Early 30s Sailing club', the name of which referred to the dates of its members births. He had a long association with the RNLI Sheringham branch, and, over a twenty-five year period, served variously as honorary secretary, deputy launching authority, committee member and chairman. As a director and treasurer of the Norfolk Boat (Sail Training) Ltd he was involved with the provision of sail training for young people, initially in the jointly owned (with the Ocean Youth Club) ketch *'Spirit of Boadicea'*, and latterly, following her sale, in craft owned by other charities.

Following his marriage and 'swallowing the anchor', he worked for a finance company of which his uncle was chairman and managing director, and after short periods in Manchester and Leeds, was sent to run the Nottingham office. Recognising that sea-going qualifications are of little value ashore, he studied and eventually qualified as a chartered secretary.

"We have two sons and a daughter, the two older of whom were born in Nottingham. Our eldest, now aged fifty-one, lives in France and runs a thoroughbred stud for the French branch of the Rothschild family, having worked similarly in Ireland. Our daughter was a lawyer and is now a part-time civil assistant district judge, whilst our youngest son is in the Norfolk police force. We have five grandchildren with a sixth on the way. I played rugby in Nottingham and agreed with a friend and fellow player that if a suitable opportunity arose we should go into business together. He heard of a sand and gravel business for sale in Norfolk and our bid for the company was successful. There was a third member of the business venture who was destined to run the sand and gravel business but he was taken ill and took no further part in its operation. Thus I was obliged to leave the finance company in 1964 and move initially to West Runton in order to take over the day-to-day running of the quarries. This was my introduction to Norfolk. The gravel quarries were in mid Norfolk and in time we received an offer from Ham and Hall River which my partners were keen to accept, and as a minority shareholder I was obliged, rather against my will, to accept also. I decided to stay with the purchasers and ran all their quarries in the eastern counties. However, they in turn were taken over by the much larger RMC, after a take over battle with Redland. RMC were well staffed and resourced and shed most of the existing Ham and Hall River staff including me.

"I was living in Norfolk and, not wanting to leave, decided to buy a farm.   It took me three years to find a suitable one at a price we could afford and, in the meantime, I developed property in Sheringham' s Uplands Park as well as working as a consultant for my former employers, the finance company, turning round a quarrying company in Cheshire which had found itself in difficulties and debt ."

"At last we found a farm of 370 acres, which was viable in those days, and grew sugar beet, cereals and potatoes.   I took all the free advice I could get from what was then the National Agricultural Advisory Service. Feeling that I would make fewer irrevocable mistakes in arable farming, it was some years before I had sufficient confidence to invest in a flock of sheep and some beef cattle.   As the shepherd, I have to say that the former provided some of the most frustrating as well as the most satisfying moments of my farming career.   However, such were the changing economics of farming that by the late 1980s the farm was too small to be sufficiently profitable and we sold it although continuing to live in one of the farmhouses which we extended and renovated.

"After a period of early retirement, I answered an advertisement for a part-time bursar three days a week at Cawston College.   It owned 120 acres of land so, in that context, I was almost able to continue farming.   The school specialised in teaching boys and girls with dyslexia and other learning difficulties but as other larger and more affluent schools met more of those needs to widen their appeal and enhance their income, Cawston lost its edge and in the face of dwindling pupil numbers, sadly closed in 1999.   I retired aged sixty-five in 2000.

"Retirement, however, was not a signal for inactivity.   I had a lot of interests and determined to pursue them.   On moving into the renovated farmhouse I had made a mental list of all the things I intended to do in the next twenty years.   Some remain uncompleted to this day as other more urgent requirements have emerged but it gets me up in the morning and there is always something to look forward to. Most of the uncompleted items on the list are physical work for which my well- equipped workshop stands ready. There is concreting to be done, paths to set out and outbuildings to repair.

"I played rugby at Holt and was treasurer of the club for a number of years before becoming for twenty years treasurer of its incorporated parent company. I also played and play golf with considerably more enthusiasm than skill and had the honour of being made captain of Sheringham Golf Club many years ago. Having married into a bridge-playing family (I came from a solo family), I started playing bridge in the 1950s and still do so regularly. I was treasurer of the Norfolk marathon during its short life and consequently involved with the Kelling Hospital Appeal. On the agricultural front for nine years I was a director of Loddon Farmers, a co-operative farmers' buying group.

"Most of my working life has been spent working independently, and, looking back, it seems my choice of careers has been largely a matter of self- indulgence. My voluntary pursuits have stemmed from an inability to say 'no' when asked to join some activity but this has led to a variety of enjoyable interests none of which I regret. However, one of the most significant changes in being retired is that I find I can and do refuse new activity if it means giving less time to my key interests. As the clock ticks on, twelve years into 'retirement' I have shed much of the load. I regret giving up farming and would like it to have continued as it was but that is wishful thinking.

"Practically my only lifelong regret is that I wish I had learned to play a musical instrument. My three older sisters had piano lessons but, when my turn came, I turned it down. As perhaps the most musical of the siblings I think it would have given me untold pleasure in later life.

"Reflecting on the above, my past reflects a certain lack of ambition, but we have been fortunate enough never to have plumbed the depths, nor faced the obligations of reaching the heights. We now enjoy our children and grandchildren, of whom we are justifiably proud."

14
Fiona Fraser

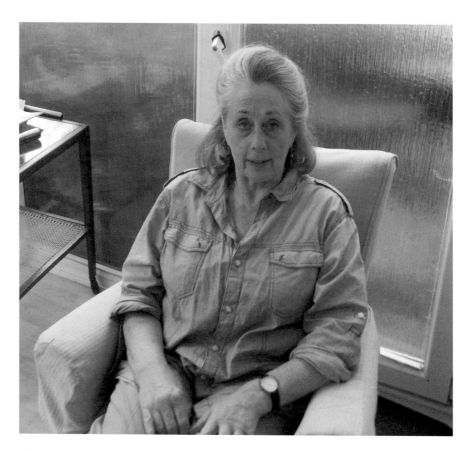

Fiona Fraser was born into an artistic family. Her father was a poet, writer painter and journalist, and her mother, Lady Margaret Douglas Home was a writer, pianist and entrepreneur. It was a natural evolution that Fiona would follow an artistic career. An early appointment was photographic archivist at the National Gallery in London, a position she held until she was expecting a family in1970.

" When I left the National Gallery I became involved in what was to become my lifetime interest in promoting contemporary music to the benefit of young composers, many of whom lived in garrets and taught in primary schools to eke out a living. They received little support or encouragement from elsewhere. Contemporary music was not well patronised and composers had the worst deal of all. I started working for the Contemporary Concerts Co-ordination, the Society for the Promotion of New Music, the Macnaghten Concerts and finally the Park Lane Group, where I continue to serve as an active member of the council. I worked for a time in the development office for Sir Neville Marriner and the Orchestra of St Martin in -the-Fields. I was also a school governor at a Catholic primary school in north London.

" Meanwhile in 1958 my family had moved from London to Burnham Market. My mother's entrepreneurial flair started the August Festival concerts and the annual Craft Fair, both of which have become local institutions. There was a tremendous enthusiasm at the time for supporting the arts and raising money for the fabric of the church. It is much more difficult today where seventy-three per cent of houses in Burnham Market are second homes and it is progressively more difficult to find volunteers.

"My husband, Sir Ian Fraser, who won the MC in the war and was awarded a CBE, retired from the chairmanship of Lazards. He wrote a book of memoirs *The High Road to England* which covered his life. Very soon after his retirement he contracted a serious heart condition. For the next ten years he needed care and nursing. I determined to keep life going and with the help of some marvellous people I started a reading group which is still functioning. We lived in an idyllic setting on a sheep farm on Exmoor. Ian died in 2003 and I moved to the family home in Burnham Market."

Fiona was no stranger to the tragedy of bereavement. Her three brothers all died in the prime of life and she offered her services to the St Joseph's Hospice in Hackney where she became a much valued bereavement visitor for them. "This was a profoundly life changing experience and my first hand knowledge of tragedy was invaluable.

"The move to Burnham Market was to be a new phase in my life. I had first visited north Norfolk in the 1950s. There is a remarkable abundance of architects, painters, sculptures, ceramicists, photographers, writers, poets, musicians and composers who choose to stay and pursue their skills here. They do so in spite of the relentlessly unfriendly wind which influences the temperature to lower than average throughout the year.

"Claims for the choice of and motives for location are many, not least selecting the remoteness and the clarity of an area not *en route* to anywhere, nor being solely a passing place. Others claim that it is easier to find a patron in north Norfolk than in other counties. There are overall attractions for the more solitary minded and mildly reclusively inclined artistic people. In north Norfolk the indigenous population offer no frills and an authenticity almost unparalleled in rural England currently. There is a suspicion, a caution and a dismissal of the intrusive incomer. The dominant certainty in the minds of the artists is the tranquillity found here. They find it possible to elevate the commonplace to convey something remarkable. The sense of space with enveloping vast skies. There is unanimous challenge found in the elusive and beguiling light. This demands from them the maximum of skills.

"Many artists return to a place which provided a haven in childhood with the idea of recapturing halcyon days. They hope the past will provide an ideal setting to develop skills thriving in the freedom of an ideally unlimited spatial background.

"I felt truly at home having moved to Burnham Market and soon became involved as co-artistic director of the Poetry Next-the-Sea Wells Festival, now in its 16th year, and an honorary advisor to the Yorke Trust for the encouragement of young musicians and singers. I have also become more and more involved as an advisory councillor of Norfolk Churches Trust. This is a massive enterprise. Norfolk has 659 medieval churches, the greatest number of any county, and it requires huge injections of capital to restore and maintain them. We raise money from donations, legacies and the generosity of the community. I am also a trustee of the League of Friends for Wells Community Hospital and honorary patron of the Northern Lights Symphony Orchestra.

"Perhaps the activity which I have found most rewarding has been the series of book launches in my house where young writers in particular find a platform to introduce their work. For many it is the first acclaim they have experienced and it is a great satisfaction to follow their success in the wider literary world. I have held thirty-four book launches to date. I also hold authors' talks where subjects have ranged from Julian of Norwich to 'Going Global'. Internationally renowned specialists on musical subjects have been invited to talk for us as part of the North Norfolk Music Festival. There is much satisfaction to be found in bringing people together who benefit from having met each other.

"Recently I have had the privilege of become involved with the Holt Festival which is having enormous success."

15
Sue and John Smart

Sue was born in Durham and educated at the girl's Grammar school there.   She went on to St Anne's College, Oxford, to read modern history, and met the man, a teacher, who was to be her first husband. Sue also qualified as a teacher and they married when she was twenty-two.   She taught at Prince William school in Oundle.   At first she found teaching in this comprehensive school an intensely depressing experience and was all for giving up but her mentor offered her the reassurance that if she stuck to it she would be fine.   Teaching was in her family and she got over the hump in a few months.   Sue resigned at the age of twenty-seven when her first child, Isabel, was born.   However this caused a big gap in the school's staffing and it was agreed that she would do a job swap with her husband.   She did not take maternity leave but limited her involvement at Oundle school to eight lessons per week.   Their second daughter, Olivia, was born two years later but soon afterwards the marriage broke up.   This was a difficult time financially and in other ways and through it all Sue continued to teach part time.

Meantime John Smart was also teaching at Oundle.   He was born in Nottingham and educated at Nottingham High school.   He went on to take a degree in English at Hertford College, Oxford.

"I then drifted around a bit and thought of myself as something of an art expert.   However, I failed to get a job at Sothebys whose interviewing panel would insist on asking me questions to which I had no answer. So I decided to become a teacher and took a postgraduate certificate in education.   At the time I was in love with a girl from Sunderland who was teaching at Orton Longueville near Peterborough.   We decided to get married and this brought us to Oundle.   The marriage did not last and gradually I came into closer contact with Sue whose marriage had also broken down, leaving her as a single mother with two daughters aged five and three.

John explains : "I was a cunning suitor and being responsible for the debating society arranged for a motion that *'A woman's place is in the home'*.   As I had hoped, this drew Sue's interest and I asked her to speak.   After which we went out to dinner.   We realised that we were both at a junction in our lives and began to spend more time together. So in 1984 we were married and I became the stepfather of two lovely daughters.

"In 1985 I was appointed head of English at Gresham's school and continued for eighteen years and then became head of arts for a further four years.   Sue took up teaching history and history of art part time at West Runton until she moved to Gresham's in 1991 to teach history."

In 1993 Sue was appointed housemistress of Oakeley, then the largest girls' house in the school and gave pastoral care and stability to 104 girls, fifty-four of whom were boarders.   Sue recalls:

"The numbers grew from eighty-four and my own girls were already there.   This caused some complications at times when as pupils they could not be shown any favours but none the less they needed me as their Mum.   I was also then child protection officer for the school. These were very fulfilling positions.

"In 1997 tragedy struck. My daughter Olivia died in a car accident and a huge piece of my life was shattered.   I carried on as housemistress until 1998 but then I felt I had to move on and do something else.   I retreated to our house in Thornage and tried to work out what I would do next.   When one loses a child the choice can be either to shut up shop and retreat from view or get on with life.   We chose the latter and I threw myself into writing."

Sue worked with the history department: "I pressed on with my project *'The School at War'* which I intended to use as material for third form history lessons. This was based on letters to the Head from

Old Greshamians who were serving in the trenches in the First World War. I involved a number of the girls to assist me in this project and as we worked we found out more and more about the boys. Those who had been lost in battle became heroes to the girls working on the project and it was very difficult for them to leave it once completed.

Eventually, in 2001, I wrote up this research as a book about a school at war, *When Heroes Die*. A few months before it came out, the journalist Richard Girling produced a powerful article based on the book. This was the lead story in the *Sunday Times Magazine*, which devoted its cover to the photographs of some of the fallen. It was unprecedented publicity and led to the BBC filming at Gresham's and in France with a moving commentary by Derek Jacobi. Working with the film crew was a very emotional experience for us all."

Sue became the deputy head of Gresham's, an appointment which went some way to correct the imbalance in that half the Gresham pupils were girls but there were no women in the senior management team. Sue continues: "The deputy head can be likened to a dean who is responsible for day to day running of a cathedral whilst the Head is more akin to a bishop. The Head's role has a bigger external dimension notably with the governors and the positioning of the school in the esteem of the outside world. Furthermore the deputy head is the link between the staff and the Head."

John retired in 2006 and Sue was asked to stay on a further two years to introduce the International Baccalaureate. This was to be done as a matter of urgency to attract more overseas boarding students to the school and to raise the academic profile. Sue explains : "I was very reluctant to take up this challenge. There was a huge administrative workload when I wanted to get back to the classroom, and I really did not think I could face it. However, the Head, Anthony Clark, persuaded me and I took it on. I hated every minute of the administration, persuasion and paperwork it entailed and after one year decided I had had enough.

"So I retired in 2007 and delighted in the illusion of freedom. I was on a high for six months. John, who had retired the year before, was less euphoric. He still felt the umbilical cord which had bound him to the School, its routines and disciplines. He also missed the company of the young. School life can make one institutionalised. The daytime is designated for work, the evenings for leisure. Neither of us could watch Television during the day although John makes the exception of televised cricket."

Sue and John have both got stuck into projects of choice. John has the strangely titled role of OG (Old Greshamian) co-ordinator and edits the OG magazine. This is published once a year and tracks many of the lives and careers of former pupils. He has published two books for Cambridge University Press on Twentieth Century British Drama and Modernism. He is currently working on *Tarantula: John Hayward, T. S. Eliot and their Circle*, due to be published later this year, which includes a survey of the London literary scene up to the 1960s. Hayward was a pupil at Gresham's at the same time as W. H. Auden, which sparked John's initial interest. Realising that he was a man of considerable influence with writers as various as Eliot, Graham Greene and Stephen Spender, but now largely forgotten, John decided to write the story of Hayward's life.

Sue took a one-year online history course to learn how computers could be used to enhance historical understanding, and earned an

Oxford University diploma in local history for which she was awarded a distinction. Her diploma was presented at the Sheldonian Theatre in Oxford. She is undertaking an ongoing project on the history of Holt 1557 to 1751. This requires study of the Holt parish registers, probate records, and church visitation records. It involves deciphering the handwriting of the parish clerks at the time. This and random spelling often resulted in near unreadable and scattered scrawl. However, the discipline of the internet has enabled historians to build up their databases and above all to access relevant material at the press of a button. "I have found this project so absorbing that I am considering extending it another century," says Sue. "Holt suffered from plague in 1592, typhoid or bubonic we do not know. In 1708 the town was devastated by fire. This gave the opportunity to rebuild it in the eighteenth century and it is one of the finest Georgian towns in the country."

Sue has also written the definitive work on George Formby. This was inspired by discussion with Richard Howard, a professional restorer of classic cars and vintage furniture, who is also the cadet force professional replicating the work of REME at the school. He knew a good deal about George Formby but acknowledged that he needed to collaborate with a skilled writer to bring it to print.

"We found there was no reliable biography of George Formby. His family were enthusiastic that we should put this right and sent us five boxes of information about him. His father had been a successful music hall star and though he died at an early age was able to provide for his family in some comfort. The image of young George Formby emerging from an impoverished background was inaccurate. He started performing often risqué songs on stage in 1925 accompanying himself on the 'banjolele', a derivative of a banjo and a ukulele invented in 1917, giving a distinctive strum."

Sue has recently been invited to become a governor of Gresham's school.

16
Martin and Peggy Swindells

Diamond wedding congratulations

Martin and his wife Peggy are both eighty-six and they continue to deliver meals on wheels to customers mostly several years younger than themselves. These same customers are fond of saying that they are getting old and recite their aches and pains but perhaps they don't realise that Martin and Peggy might well be returning from taking patients to and from medical treatment in hospital. Their level of activity is truly amazing and impressive.

Born in 1926 in Bolton, Martin had a brother and a sister and numerous cousins with whom they holidayed at the seaside in Wales. In 1939 Martin entered the Royal Naval College, Dartmouth, and served in the

Navy until 1953. In 1949 he married Peggy whom he had met at the Chelsea Arts Ball. They were both twenty-three. Her father practised as a GP in Hampshire.

"I worked my way up to Lieutenant Commander and found teaching sub- lieutenants kindled my enthusiasm to make teaching my career. We had two children by this time and the Navy offered me a shore job so I could spend time with my family. However, helpful as the intention was, in reality my schedule demanded that I leave home on a Sunday afternoon returning home on the following Saturday morning. So I decided on a career change study for a degree and become a housemaster at a public school. However, I was encouraged to pursue a teaching career in the prep school world. The necessary qualification could be obtained by taking up a three-year course which would run concurrently with practical experience and I taught at West Hill prep school in Hampshire. In 1960 I replied to an advertisement to buy Beeston Hall school in north Norfolk. Many prep schools in those days were privately owned and the owner was the headmaster. Peggy and I were attracted by this prospect with a view to establishing charitable status for the school in due course. This would be a major transition. Until then the headmaster/owner was the authority and had to pay himself out of the proceeds of the school. However, in charitable status a board of directors was appointed and took on the responsibility. They appointed the headmaster and paid him a salary.

"Peggy and I went to look at the school and its location. The weather was really hostile and Peggy said if I took up the appointment she would give me five years and not one day more. The role of the Headmaster's wife at a prep school was pivotal. We stayed for twenty-six years after the first six of which in 1966 we achieved our goal of charitable status and my appointment as headmaster was constantly renewed. Over time we developed the school from boys only to co-ed. Beeston Hall was in a run down state with just fifty pupils when we took it on. We built it up to 180 over the years to come. The county took a generous view of supporting the cost of education. Once a pupil had passed the eleven-plus Norfolk paid for all his or her education. We lived all-found at the school which enabled us to take just a token salary until we became a charitable trust. I was fortunate in having served in the Royal Navy at a time when it was trying to shrink its numbers and had taken up the generous gratuity and pension scheme on offer.

"We had 100 boarders and eighty daily boarders. The latter could sleep in the school during the week if they chose and do their prep there in the evening. This reduced the divide between day boys and boarders.

I chose to retire at the age of sixty in 1986 and pondered whether or not to take another job. We felt a sense of achievement in our work at Beeston Hall. But surprisingly, having laid down the load I did not miss it having other things to think about. Two days after retiring from the school I had both hips replaced and this took six months to be fully operational. I decided to have both done at the same time. This was preferable, I was assured, to having one done and then the other, thus dragging out the process to the point where I might never have gone in for the second one. It was a great success.

"Peggy had become much involved with Riding for the Disabled in the 1970s and although she retired from active participation with the horses when she was seventy-five her skills as an accomplished needlewoman keeps her busy sewing and knitting for fundraising sales. Also for eight years she worked in the Sue Ryder shop in Holt until she had a hip operation which curtailed her activities at least for a while.

"Two months after I stepped down from Beeston Hall I invited one of our bridesmaids to lunch at the Hoste Arms. She was aged sixty and still beautiful. A former parent at Beeston approached me and suggested that I must miss the school to which I answered 'not in the least'. His surprise was matched only by the realisation that my lunch guest was not my wife. He said to me out of the corner of his mouth as we stood at the bar for drinks 'that hip operation seems to have worked wonders for you.' This gave Peggy and me some amusement.

"We moved to a house in Gunthorpe where I pursued my love of gardening. But I came to the conclusion that retired people need something to do. Peggy and I played bridge socially for a penny a hundred. It is an effective way to meet people and has no retirement age. I had been honorary secretary of the Sheringham lifeboat for ten years. My duties included command of the boathouse and weekly drilling on the beach. We had a large lifeboat and I had to authorise every launch which I could do on the phone from Gunthorpe six miles from the boathouse. However, reorganisation of the lifeboat service meant that Sheringham exchanged its large boat for a smaller beach-launched craft. The local sea conditions had to be inspected before it was launched and this was impractical from Gunthorpe so I had to retire from the job.

"For two years I toured schools encouraging fundraising support for the 'Back the Track' charity. This was raising money to finance the construction of an athletics track until it was put on hold and I retired again. A fruit farmer, Michael Buckingham, father of two of the pupils at Beeston had arranged to give them a Christmas treat seeing a show in London. When they came out of the theatre the daughter was shocked at the number begging in the street and this was in the run-up to Christmas. Michael agreed to supply his produce to what became Crisis at Christmas and arranged for other farmers and food contacts to do the same. However, such was the response that food came in such profusion that it generated waste. Michael decided that it should be better organised.

"I was put in charge of raising contributions from schools and found that there was a greater willingness to donate goods e.g sugar, than cash. This was gratefully received. Eventually Crisis at Christmas extended its activities all the year round and became known as Crisis. I was involved for over ten years until I retired again.

"At Gunthorpe in 1986 there were few people prepared to do much for the church. The Church of England congregation was down to ten having split from the Methodists. This was out of 120 residents. Peggy and I were 'Shanghaied' on to the PCC. I became secretary and treasurer. A recent survey of the church fabric building had revealed that the tower needed expenditure of £30,000 to save it. With the dynamic leadership and generosity of the wife of the owner of Gunthorpe Hall, Peggy and I joined the Friends of Gunthorpe Parish and with considerable effort we raised the money through donations, fetes and coffee mornings.

"The Arthritis and Rheumatism Council (ARC) in north Norfolk were active but in need of funds. Peggy, who became the chair and I joined the committee and were responsible for collecting boxes.

"We moved to Holt in 2005 and discovered the Holt Area Caring Society, set up by the Holt practice senior partner and developed into a service for taking people for medical treatment. They needed volunteer car drivers. When I was eighty I suggested that my driving should be assessed and I was tested successfully by very helpful ex-police driving instructors. Now eighty-six I continue to do so. We volunteers operated on a centrally controlled roster giving us journeys for local, intermediate and long distance journeys. I have only had one nasty person in all the years I have been driving for the scheme : a rather self important lady emerged as the customer who had an appointment at the hospital. On the return journey she asked (told) me to stop at a bank as she needed to draw some money. This amounted to £500. When we reached her home I asked her, as is customary with all passengers, if she would like to make a donation to the scheme and I indicated that £5 was the usual amount. She burst into fury and fished in her bag for 55p which she threw at me before flouncing off. This was reported to our controller and when she requested further help the service was always fully occupied and could not oblige her.

"One October Peggy and I saw a WRVS advertisement in the *Chronicle* for drivers for meals on wheels. This got bogged down in bureaucracy until the following spring because the secretary had signed in blue ink rather than black.

"In my teaching career I produced plays at school. My favourite was *My Fair Lady*. I preferred producing to acting and I certainly could not sing. As a child I was detailed to go to French lessons rather than prove again that my singing voice was below par."

Peggy and Martin have been married for sixty-three years. For their Golden Wedding they went on a Baltic cruise and for their Diamond Wedding they travelled to Australia to visit family.

"Our eldest daughter is an advisor on people in homes to which they have been sent by the courts and this involves mainly mental health work.

Three generations

Our middle daughter was headhunted by Richard Branson to Virgin Bank. She had worked with the Royal Bank of Scotland which took her to Scotland four days a week. Our youngest daughter organises teaching of people with learning difficulties. We have seven grandchildren and two great grandchildren.

"I have been lucky in life, notably the twenty years that have followed retirement age."

17.
Geof Hanley

Born and brought up in Plymouth with a great love of being out in the wilds of Dartmoor, Geof assumed in the fullness of time he would retire back to the West Country. However, his life has taken up new challenges and unexpected opportunities.

"I was destined to go to Leeds University when I left school at eighteen to read chemical engineering but three weeks before end of term I picked up a book on international banking which talked about eighteen month tours in the Middle East followed by four months paid leave. As the money was considerably more than I could hope to earn in the short and medium-term as a chemical engineer, I applied and got a job working for the Eastern Bank, a subsidiary of the Chartered Bank, which is now the Standard Chartered Group. During my time with them, I spent a year on secondment with three other single twenty year old chaps working in the Hamburg branch of Chartered Bank. Interesting times. It also coincided with England winning the World Cup in 1966. You can imagine what the atmosphere in the office was like the following Monday morning...

"At twenty-one when I was due to go on my first major tour to the Middle East, I asked permission to get married and they said no. At that time it was one of the rules that you had to travel as a single man as taking a new wife unfamiliar with the overseas colonial lifestyle could prove very difficult.

Therefore I had to resign from the Chartered Bank and joined Midland Bank working in their international division branches in Bristol, London, Liverpool and Cardiff. This is where I started to learn how to manage people, the hardest part of any job, particularly as I was thirty years younger than many of the staff in the branches. I gravitated back to London, ironically to cover the Middle East and north Africa offering the international trade services of Midland to all major banks in the area. This coincided with the oil price hike in the early 1970's and so business was booming in that part of the world.

"In the late 1970s I spent two years living and working in Iran for Midland Bank and had to leave rather abruptly, due to the revolution, in the same week as the Shah.

"Following my ten year stint travelling to a number of Middle East and north African countries I migrated through several other areas of the bank including financial control, operations, electronic banking and credit cards. During this time along came HSBC who bought Midland and brought with them a different culture and ways of doing business. My last few years at HSBC were, in part, spent looking after external third party relationships and negotiating commercial contracts with them.

"In 1997 I had the option to retire for the first time at the age of fifty-one which I took. However, I had no intention of actually retiring and started to consider what options were available. As in many businesses, it's as much "who you know" as "what you know", and I was invited (through a contact at HSBC) to talk to a senior manager in Prudential Banking. He was looking at a new banking service which many months later was launched as the virtual on-line bank called "EGG".

"I was originally invited as a consultant for twelve months but ended up staying for eight years becoming one of their negotiators of major contracts covering in particular operational platforms for savings and credit cards, insurance, investments etc. and finally debt collectors.

"By now, having turned sixty, I decided to look for part-time work and over the next three years secured a number of contracts all coming through contacts within the financial services industry, including a business development plan for a debt collecting agency followed by mortgage valuations with my finale being working for an Icelandic Bank which was then put into receivership as the world recession hit right in the middle of my contract…what an unspectacular end to my professional life…

"In parallel with my time at EGG, my wife Suzanne and I had been thinking about spending weekends away from east London, where we then lived, and although I had expected to be looking further west, as the first step to returning to the West Country, I was persuaded to head east up the M11 to look at Suffolk/Norfolk.

"We started at Southwold and over the next few weekends gravitated further and further northwards up East Anglia until we ran out of land. One of the house circulars we looked at was for a small modern bungalow in Kestrel Close, Burnham Market, which in fact we bought in June 2000 without really seeing the centre of the village and having no idea of its attraction and fame.

"We came to Norfolk every weekend for the next couple of years, spending many happy early Sunday mornings on Holkham beach marvelling at the fact we were the only ones there (well it was 6.00 am) – quite a contrast to life around London.

"By now we had realised that Burnham Market ,and the surrounding area and coastline, was a great place to be and we decided this was where we would like to retire. So we looked for a more permanent home, which we soon found in the village, and have now lived here for 1ten years full-time. Absolutely the best decision we have made (except for getting married of course !).

"For my sins, as Suzanne and her mother Hylda were very close, we asked her to join us up here in Norfolk. Hylda soon settled in to village life and in recent years had been living in Polstede Place until last year reaching the grand age of ninety-four. It then became necessary for her to be cared for 24/7 and is now residing happily in a care home in Hunstanton.

"Although when we first moved here full time, with potential retirement on the horizon, I was still working four days a week at EGG in Derby, I began to consider how I could become more integrated and involved in life in the village, with Suzanne hinting at council work. At that time the Village Plan and in particular the long running saga of a potential car park were high on the agenda. So I thought it would be good to try and get on to the parish council to be at the centre of things.

"A vacancy came up – some seven years ago – and I was co-opted. Great I thought now I can get involved in the car park project. However, as mother-in-law at that time moved into Polstede Place I had what is called a 'prejudicial interest' and could not take part in the discussions. This has recently changed, in fact since Hylda has gone into the care home and Polstede Place was sold so I can at last get involved, after all these years, in the car park project.

"For the past five years I have been Chair of the parish council and whilst I very much enjoy the ability to help plan for and look after the future of Burnham Market and its residents/visitors you soon learn that you can't please everyone all of the time. Now and again would be good. There are still a number of ongoing challenges facing the council and the biggest and probably the one with the greatest long- term impact on the village is the potential car park/toilets.

"Alongside becoming a councillor and still during my time working at EGG in Derby I learned that Anne Cringle and Yvonne King, who had given many loyal years to running the annual Craft Fair in Burnham Market were looking to "retire" and if no-one filled their shoes the Fair would not take place.

"Suzanne again suggested I might consider getting involved and as I think the Craft Fair is a great event in the village I went along to a meeting to volunteer my services as did a chap called Bob Lamont. We hit it off right away and so started a partnership including Lawrence Rubin (the new treasurer) which has continued for the past six years. Demand for stalls grows year on year and I believe the Fair is as popular as ever and one of the key events in the village calendar.

"As if that wasn't enough I was volunteered by Suzanne (they do say behind every great man is an even greater woman) to help find speakers for the Gardening Club which I have been doing for the past couple of years. It has been really interesting chatting to a number of potential speakers who have a very wide range of interests and topics about which they will talk.

Craft fair

"Then came the Queen's Diamond Jubilee celebration in the village within which I was also involved in the planning and organisation of the day.

"So, as you can see, retirement as such hasn't really happened yet and I often wonder how I ever found time to go to work at all.

"Possibly time to slow down a bit (?) and focus more on things that Suzanne and I would like to do. Walking in Norfolk is a real treat and when the weather is fine you might even see us cycling. A few years ago I did the Norwich 100 mile bike event. Suzanne asked me how much of the countryside I saw… didn't... as I just had my head down and concentrated on getting to the finish.

"We have been to South Africa a number of times to see Suzanne's son Ian who lives in Cape Town and on one visit I did the Argus – a very well known cycle ride (if you are a cyclist), a sixty-seven mile up and down mountainous course. Tough but immensely rewarding as this time I did look around and the scenery was breathtaking.

"So, what of the immediate future ?

"Burnham Market certainly has its challenges particularly if we are to preserve the best of the village atmosphere. With over seventy per cent of houses being second homes this is not going to be easy. Also catering for the ever growing number of tourists/visitors brings its own problems.

"With potential relaxation of planning restrictions there will be a number of housing development proposals emerging not only relating to the potential car park project but also on other pockets of land in and around the village.

"Will I stay involved?...probably…maybe scale it back a bit.

"Do Suzanne and I still really love living in Burnham Market?…yes we do. We have many friends in the village and feel very fortunate to be able to live in our lovely home in this special part of the country.

"But…I fancy one last personal project which would involve a smaller house but with more land, so who knows what will emerge in the future".

18
Robert Hill

Born in Hackney Robert was the only child of working class parents who through hard work and determination both achieved key positions at the top of small companies.

"My father started in Covent Garden fruit and vegetable market and became Managing Director of a fruit and veg company. My mother was in the rag trade and ended up managing that business. I went to the local Church of England primary school and by the age of ten I was in the church choir and starting piano lessons. At secondary school I disliked and had no aptitude for sport preferring to study music and become proficient at the piano. This tended to drive me apart from other boys who had no interest in music and I suffered as Billy Elliot must have done for being different from the run of the mill. This did not help my confidence. But I had a stubborn streak and was fortunate to have teachers who recognised and respected separate talents in their pupils and spent time encouraging them to use their aptitude. This inspired me to respect the talent of individuals and to look to teaching music as a career.

"I went on to Trinity College of Music in London. I was the first member of my wider family to move into higher education and although my parents were supportive of the idea they were nonetheless scared and nervous. What if it all went wrong what would I fall back on for a career? So I went to work as a clerk at the Royal Docks and at the Stratford International Freight Terminal. This was to become the site of the 2012 Olympic Games. I hated the work but stuck it for two years. It was a valuable experience of the real world and looking back I realise I benefited from it.

"Trinity College was a shock. After tmy cosy secondary school it was a totally different environment where many of the students were more confident, middle class, better educated and better off. They were more certain of their place in life. However I soon learnt to progress, that stubborn streak again. In my four years studying at the College I became competent as a pianist, organist and conductor. After graduating I went on to a year of teacher training and then taught music in large comprehensive schools in the East End of London. Inevitably there was the struggle to persuade young people – particularly at that time - that music was for all who had or who could develop the talent. The growth of pop music helped to change attitudes. The Inner London Education Authority was providing excellent resources in musical education and the school had a big music department with lots of instruments.

Although I was a new teacher in East London I continued my professional musical life by accompanying fine choirs and conducting performances of Bach's St Matthew Passion and St John Passion at Southwark Cathedral,the South Bank and Royal Albert Hall. I also took over an Opera Group in Richmond, Surrey conducting Mozart and Britten operas. It was varied and very hard work. Teaching in the day and performing in the evenings was a tiring and demanding schedule.

"By the time I was in my mid thirties it was decision time. I gave up my head of music post and took on more part time, freelance work. At this time I was also accompanying singers and instrumentalists is a variety of concerts. I've always loved working with other musicians. The piano and organ can be lonely instruments. Sharing ideas in rehearsals and working as a pair or team is particularly rewarding. However I found I had very little for myself or even time to enjoy the work I was doing.

"During this time I met other teachers who, through inspirational ideas, re-awakened my commitment to teaching in schools. In my late 30s I was appointed to the Head of Music post in a school in West London. There was a varied cross section of students and stimulating colleagues with whom to discuss teaching methods and approaches. Out of this I became Head of Performing Arts and Senior Teacher Music is physically demanding and in my early forties I decided to apply for a post in Senior Management in Schools. I was very interested in developing the curriculum to meet the needs of students, not just academically but also personally. At this time the new National Curriculum was introduced, spear headed by Kenneth Baker. I became deputy head of a very large school in Tower Hamlets with its challenging mixture of cultures. I still did some teaching although my main responsibilities were designing the curriculum and dealing with all the other management and leadership tasks that the job entailed. I was very happy in my job particularly when I became involved in the professional development of teachers and training new teachers. There was little time though for a personal life let alone musical life!

"Around the turn of the century there was a focus on the need for independent schools to become more involved with the community. State schools were partnered with independent schools in local areas and I became involved in organising and running courses on leadership issues. This made an impact on both sectors. Working with teachers who were focused on exams in their subjects and with students who were required to became similarly focused tended to breed enclosed communities who forgot the outside world. It was rewarding and challenging to widen that focus. Conversely teachers in the state sector learnt much from independent school colleagues on A level teaching and application to university for young people.

"My father died aged sixty-six in 1987 and in 1988 I bought a holiday cottage in Rogers Row, Burnham Market.   By 2003 I was fortunate to be offered early retirement/redundancy on favourable terms.   The local authority tended to select the more expensive teachers for this programme and I was expensive!   We came to a favourable deal and I retired to Norfolk at the age of fifty-four although I would carry on part time as an education consultant specialising on School Leadership and Teacher Training. I applied to the Norfolk County Council to become a school governor and was appointed to Alderman Peel High School in Wells where I am now vice chairman.

"Retirement was a releasing experience.   For the first time in my career I could say 'No' to offered commitments.   I did not have to please any boss other than myself. I did not want to be immersed in regular commitments such as a church organist for which there is always a strong demand.   For the first time I could get away on holiday in September – my preferred month.   The USA is a favourite destination. I could make choices and give a new purpose to my life, continuing however in the field where I felt most comfortable but I did not want to do too much.   One of my new fulfilments was to be involved in the production and rehearsals for the pantomimes in North Creake as musical director as well as acting in plays. "

Robert is an accomplished cook and gets continual inspiration from going out to restaurants, concerts and theatres. He really appreciates the hard work that goes into the "finished product".   His leading and most admired composer is Wagner.   What would be his reaction if he were invited to conduct the Ring Cycle at Bayreuth?   "Yes I would be tempted to accept"

19
About the Author

Raymond Monbiot was born in Kent in 1937 and educated at Westminster School. He taught Latin, history and English at a prep school. In 1956 he entered the food industry as a trainee with J Lyons, humping sacks of flour in the basement. These were formative years in understanding people. By the age of nineteen he was foreman on the night shift when the foreman had authority, in later years delegated to the human resources department. The foreman had responsibility for the motivation of employees, many of them casual, who had enrolled for the night from the local doss house in Hammersmith, looking for an opportunity to sleep in the warm rather than work. The factory was a Victorian building six storeys high and in the course of his duties he was the target of a 44lb tin of frozen egg thrown from the roof and of a 500lb barrel of fat rolled down the stairs. Both missed their target but made an indelible impression none the less. Despite these incidents involving the drifters, the challenge was to get the job done to time and standard and the loyalty and dedication of the many long-term employees was truly impressive. The war had not long ended and family men and women were trying to recreate some stability and normality. It was a humbling but indispensable experience to learn that security and recognition for effort are the best motivators.

He was trained as a pastry chef making cakes for Buckingham Palace garden parties and fruit scones for the Queen Mother's breakfast (by hand). He chose to move on to the sales side of the business and started as a van salesman selling and delivering cake to a round of shops. He worked his way up the sales ladder to sales director and eventually ran three food companies for Lyons as managing director After twenty-two years he was headhunted to be managing director of Associated Biscuits, that is Jacobs, Peek Freans and Huntley and Palmers. In 1982 he moved to Campbells Soups as chairman UK and in 1988 founded his own food consultancy business.

He was an active member of the Conservative party for over fifty-four years and held every volunteer position except chairman of the women's organisation. He was the senior volunteer 2003 to 2006 and deputy chairman of the party, and from 2006 to 2011, a treasurer and chairman of its property company. Awarded MBE 1981 and CBE 1994. Declined a life peerage 2010. The years involved with the Conservative party brought him into contact with every one of its Leaders, since Winston Churchill, and many senior ministers. The cut and thrust of parliamentary debate has not improved since television made it into popular entertainment encouraging 'yah boo' politics. Memorable repartee, however, remains in his mind. "Harold Macmillan was being taunted by a northern railwayman MP about hunting and shooting. He thanked the MP for his observations but said he would value his opinion more on shunting and hooting. Iain Mcleod, one of the great losses to politics through his early death, proposed a bargain with one of his tormentors:- 'You stop telling lies about me and I'll stop telling the truth about you.' And Margaret Thatcher addressing the Conservative party conference said 'Mr Chairman, the last Labour Government and I do mean the last Labour Government...' However the sharpest lines were by no means monopolised by the Conservatives as witness the barbs of Dennis Skinner, the Beast of Bolsover.

"One of the most exacting tasks was to chair the Conservative party conference in the year 2000. With thousands in the hall and many more watching on television the challenge over four days was to get the audience on side and keep them there. One splendid councillor addressing the gathering started her speech with 'You don't frighten me, I've got children...' There were 300,000 members of the party in those days with many different opinions about what should be done. However, there was an overwhelming, unifying loyalty. In my three years as chairman of the volunteers there were three Leaders and four party Chairman, each of whom expected a transfer of that loyalty in their direction – not an easy task at times."

Married to Rosalie Monbiot OBE they have two surviving children: George, a well known environmentalist who writes for *The Guardian*, and Eleanor, a senior director of World Vision who lives in Kenya and was awarded the OBE at the age of thirty-four. Their daughter Katherine died at the age of thirty-one. Raymond and Rosalie moved to Norfolk in 2000. Rosalie was elected a Norfolk county councillor and to the parish council. Raymond became president of the North West Norfolk Conservative Association. They planted an orchard of heritage apple trees at their home in Burnham Market and are keenly interested in cultivating them. They established a unique burr knot tree, that is one resulting from a cutting rather than from grafting, and it is likely to produce apples unlike the variety from which the cutting was obtained. This planting produced just such an apple and it was named Canon Cooke after Rosalie's brother.

They celebrated their Golden Wedding with the help of a hundred friends in 2011. Raymond is a published author. His first book *'How to Manage Your Boss'* sold 30,000 copies. He was a regular contributor to trade magazines and since moving to Norfolk writes features on interesting people for *North Norfolk Living.* He has written three books about Norfolk characters for whom he has a lot of respect. The first was *The Burnhams Book of Characters*, followed by *Characters of North Norfolk* and by *MORE Characters of North Norfolk.* He contributed a chapter to *The Return of the Tide,* and was one of the team who wrote *The Book of the Burnhams.* This latest book *Retirement is for Younger People* reflects his respect for the volunteers who carry on contributing to the community regardless of their age.

A former chairman of the Burnhams Society, he is a keen gardener and specialises in roses as far as the soil and climate allow. Wherever they have lived they have planted a mulberry tree. He has won numerous prizes for rose growing and he and Rosalie encourage barn owls and hedgehogs at Eastgate House, Burnham Market.